WHEN
YOUR
MIND
SCREAMS

WHEN YOUR MIND SCREAMS

FINDING PEACE AND CONFIDENCE IN THE MIDST OF ANXIETY

CHRISTOPHER GLATIS

WHEN YOUR MIND SCREAMS
Finding Peace and Confidence in the Midst of Anxiety

ISBN   978-1-5445-3540-1   *Hardcover*

        978-1-5445-3538-8   *Paperback*

        978-1-5445-3539-5   *Ebook*

CONTENTS

To all of you that struggle with anxiety and think there is no way out.
This is for you. I am on your side and here to tell you there is a way
you can break free and learn to appreciate your anxiety.
You will. I have no doubt. Let's do this together.

PROLOGUE

YOU ARE NOT
ALONE

HOW I GOT HERE

I REMEMBER IT SO VIVIDLY. I WAS SITTING IN THE BACK OF A CAR WITH friends, riding from Ocean City, Maryland, to Dewey Beach, Delaware. Suddenly, my body went into fight-or-flight mode. My chest tightened so furiously it knocked the wind out of me, as though there were a three-thousand-pound boulder on my chest. My mind was screaming, too many thoughts and nothing to slow down their speed or intensity. *What's going on? Am I having a heart attack? Am I actually going to die during beach week? At eighteen? Can my friends see what's going on inside of me? Somebody…help me.*

As I looked around at my friends, they had smiles on their faces; they were laughing and didn't seem to have a care in the world. We had graduated high school two days before, and they were celebrating the end of one stage of their lives as they moved toward the next. They were embracing it; I could not. I didn't have time to be jealous of their joy and excitement because I was terrified, frozen in the grips of something spiraling out of control. They had no idea terrifying physical and psychological side effects were tearing me apart from the inside. Since I didn't want my friends to realize what was going on, I did my best to engage in the conversation, but I could hardly string a sentence together. I was trying to leave my body.

This sort of thing, this terror, was something I certainly didn't want to admit to anyone, including myself. I was a man, or becoming a man, and I was supposed to be tough. And I thought reaching out for help, expressing my feelings, was not the safe path. I thought it was a weak choice. And I was not weak.

So, I basically overrode what I was experiencing. I white-knuckled the rest of the car ride, and when we arrived at our destination, I jumped onto the sand-strewn parking lot, sun blinding my eyes and poker face in full effect. Inside, I was trembling, gasping for breath. I knew, I was certain, something was terribly wrong with me. Possibly unfixable. And I wanted to tell someone. But I couldn't. That would just make things worse.

I was a mess. During my final year of high school, I had felt as though I was slipping into a dark abyss. It was much more than just not feeling like myself. Now, looking back, I believe I was entering the early stages of depression.

This had been building for a long time, just underneath the surface.

I had been struggling with the "not good enough" syndrome for quite some time. I wasn't really a great student, experimented with drugs, got into trouble quite a bit, and upon graduation, I really didn't fully believe that I would be able to survive in college or the real world that followed soon after. I had a lot of fear around taking that next step. I did not trust myself—or anyone else, for that matter.

So, during beach week, a time that was supposed to be about letting loose and celebrating the end of high school with my fellow classmates, I had my first full-blown panic attack.

What I now know is this anxiety, and, in turn, depression, had been brewing for years, and I hadn't been aware of it. I definitely wasn't going to tell anyone how I *felt*. Feelings weren't respected in my family. Most likely, this behavior around emotional sharing, or lack thereof, was passed down to my mother and father from the people who raised them. Then, they kept the cycle going with my sister and me. I truly believed feelings, *my feelings*, could be used against me.

This life change, going from high school to college, was my breaking point. It was the match to my dynamite fuse. It meant separation from everything I knew. My girlfriend, my friends, my surroundings, my comfort zone, my life as I knew it.

When I set off for college in a small eastern town in North Carolina, I felt even more unsafe. I was with strange, new people in a strange land. All my suppressed and unaddressed emotions swirled up and created a dark soup that enveloped me in fear. I didn't even know what the different emotions I was feeling were or what they felt like individually, and that uncertainty about *what* I was feeling only exacerbated the fear. My anxiety skyrocketed. This new environment, the new way of life, the uncertainty, the expectations tied to academic performance, only fed my anxiety. I started having regular panic attacks in the classroom.

I went to college because that was "what you do" after high school, but I was so lost. I was looking for answers to my stress and anxiety that no one up to this point, including my parents, had been willing to give me. From my father, I usually got, "Go to the gym," or "It's nothing, you're just thinking too much." The most insidious advice I got was from a family doctor who told me to drink a glass of wine or "Just take this Xanax."

When I had had enough, much to my type-A father's chagrin, I tracked down a local psychiatrist. I needed answers, and at that point, I was willing to do anything to get them.

My father was old-school Greek Orthodox. He grew up on the rough streets of East Boston, ran "errands" for a local mobster to contribute to his family's income, and basically came from nothing. He was proud and strict. He believed life is tough, and you need to meet that toughness with toughness. I wanted to make him proud. I wanted him to love me. So admitting to some sort of defect in myself and committing to a plan to deal with it that was the exact opposite of his idea of how I should handle things was confusing for me and created a lot of fear and a lack of trust in myself.

Inside, I was deteriorating. I felt so much embarrassment and shame. I felt broken. I hid my ordeal from everyone. I was certain something was seriously defective within me.

At that time, in 1985, the word on anxiety disorders really hadn't hit the streets just yet. The American Psychiatric Association had only recognized generalized anxiety disorder as a diagnosis in 1980, and it was thought to be way more common in women. That just made things worse, as it fed my insecurities about what it meant to be a man.

Within five minutes of our first session, the shrink said, "You have panic disorder." And the crazy thing is he said it calmly, with a smile.

For the first time in my life, the veil of shame momentarily lifted, and I felt profound relief. I felt I had finally found someone who understood me. The emotional pain I was feeling constantly, that was eating away at my core, had a name. And other people had this disorder too. I did not feel so alone anymore.

My psychiatrist proceeded to load me up on antidepressants and "as-needed" benzodiazepines, then sent me on my way.

I will say that shrink and those meds were saviors. I was willing to put up with cottonmouth; mood swings; wild, frightening dreams; drowsiness; my own belief that taking medications was a weakness; and, ironically, more anxiety symptoms, to get some relief. The anxiety and panic attacks subsided.

I was able to live with these trade-offs for a bit, but then, toward the end of my undergraduate college years—and an extended period of feeling "normal"—something inside me told me I didn't need the meds anymore. It wasn't really a voice; it was more a feeling. I will also say I continued to struggle with the fact that I needed this crutch in the first place. So I got a bit brave. I hesitantly went off the meds. And for a good stretch, I did very well. Then, I entered graduate film school, and the ugly symptoms of fear, dread, and a debilitating lack of trust in myself and the world returned. The self-doubt and other negative emotions felt way too big for my human body to contain. However, now I could see a pattern.

Change and uncertainty equaled anxiety.

After I had settled into the routine of this new scholastic endeavor, the anxiety subsided once again, and I intuitively felt that meds were not right for me and that I certainly could get along without them. I discontinued them. Since then, for the last twenty-five years, I've been psych-med free.

This "disease" is insidious. It will tear you down from the inside out and make your life a living hell. *If* you allow it to.

Anxiety disorders create a complete lack of trust in the physical body, the mind, and, ultimately, the world around you. Over those brutal and uncertain years, I thought:

- I was dying from cancer (all kinds), a heart attack, a stroke, or multiple sclerosis.

- I was losing my mind; I had slipped into dementia or Alzheimer's.

- I was in the early stages of manic depression, psychosis, or schizophrenia.

- I was losing my hearing and my eyesight.

- Unchecked tooth decay would lead to some sort of dangerous and deadly disease.

- I had Tourette's syndrome.

- I might do something dangerous to others or myself.

- If I got too close to the edge of a tall building's rooftop, I might jump.

- This torture I was experiencing would never stop.

And *none* of the above has happened or most likely ever *will* happen in my lifetime.

I even questioned my sexuality because the turmoil inside caused me to doubt who I was.

Well, the torture has finally stopped.

Now, as a grown man in a wonderful marriage with careers in the entertainment industry and international business ventures, I have the tools and insights that come with managing the trials of living. I no longer view my anxiety as a disorder. I call it "a challenge." Being a writer, I know how powerful words can be, and there is no use cementing an idea that just isn't true. Anxiety is a challenge, not a disorder.

Hispano-Roman Stoic philosopher, statesman, and dramatist Seneca the Younger said, "He is most powerful who has power over himself."[1] I believe he was saying that until we know ourselves deeply, unearth the causes behind the symptoms, and make peace with all our parts, which then allows us to *be* with all of it, the joy and the terror, we are susceptible to the whims of the world.

Initially, I grabbed on tight and tried to control *everything* in my life, which only exacerbated the exact thing, anxiety, that I was trying to run away from.

Here's one thing I know for certain. In all the years I've experienced panic and anxiety, they really never go away. I've read a zillion books and articles on this subject and practiced all sorts of anti-anxiety modalities (from meditation to psychedelic therapy), and anxiety still lurks, waiting for me to drop my guard, to believe it, to feed it.

I have heard people say they've cured their anxiety. It's completely gone. Just like magic. I call bullshit.

I'm not saying it's not possible. I'm saying I believe it's rare.

Life will always be there to throw you curveballs and upsets. Anxiety and stress are part of life. We sufferers may experience them on a much more intense level than most people, but whether you are clinically challenged or not, anxiety and stress will always be there on some level.

I know that is probably not what you want to hear, but you should know it up front.

The key is how you respond to your anxiety.

As I write this right now, I have a low level of fear about my physical well-being. My chest is a bit tight, and I'm wondering how much longer I have on this planet. That's right. After all the work I've done, tentacles of anxiety are still there, slithering, simmering, testing me.

So then, why am I writing this book? Why don't I just stop now and say, "Good luck, people, because you are ultimately fucked"?

Because even though every day I experience some sort of uneasiness tied to this *challenge* I have, I believe, over the years, anxiety has also become my friend, my ally, and, maybe, just maybe, my greatest teacher.

It has pushed me to do and experience things I never would have done without it. It has made me a whole person, three dimensional.

So if I can tame the beast, you can too. We can live fulfilling lives with it.

We can live deeper lives.

We can turn it into fuel.

Yes, I know it sounds crazy. But if your goal is to befriend it and not annihilate it—to sit with it, to learn from it—I think we all have a better chance of success.

Keep your friends close and your enemies closer, right?

I'm going to show you how you can live with anxiety. How you can pull it closer instead of push it away and, through that act, minimize it. And if you can't minimize it, you can learn to dance with it. And in that dance, you take away its power. You will know yourself on a level you never thought possible.

My hope is you come away with something, even if it is *one* small tool or insight, that takes the edge off this thing we call anxiety, fear, worry, concern, and terror.

To me, that is success.

YOUR STORY

You are scared, you are confused, you are frustrated, and you may have given up all hope. You may have even held up two middle fingers to the world around you and said, "Fuck it all, I'm done. This shit is going to be with me forever." I know the feeling. And let me guess, you've read books, articles, and blog posts about anxiety and became more confused than before you read them. Maybe you've even read a piece that opens up exactly the way this chapter has, and you're wondering whether this book will be more of the same copy-paste anxiety advice. I know your plight. This book is for YOU.

Anxiety exists to keep you scared, confused, angry, powerless, and feeling sorry for yourself and, ultimately, convince you to give up. These feelings fuel anxiety. Because anxiety doesn't want to die. It wants to stay alive to keep you safe. So you see, its mission is to help, but it's actually doing anything but.

I wrote this book for anxiety sufferers who have tried everything and are ready and willing to learn how to lean into their anxieties and fears instead of avoiding them. Unlike other books out there, these chapters won't focus on how to destroy or control your anxiety. Instead, this book offers relief and a solid plan, a way forward, that enables you to live with and embrace your anxiety and, in turn, minimize it. Since I am a creative, I also explore the unique ways anxiety can wreak havoc on artists. The fact that art is so subjective sets us up for a lot of rejection, disappointment, fear, and anxiety.

I am here to tell you that whatever your background, however you developed your particular flavor of anxiety, you can and *will* come out of this dense, scary fog a richer, deeper, more confident, and more well-rounded human being. Knowing that you can face these inner demons and come out the other side will give you the courage to face so much in life. You may have hit rock bottom, or you may have just had your first panic attack. It doesn't matter. You can evolve your relationship with it all. In fact, the relationship you have with anxiety is your key to getting past it.

With all that being said, I know this book is not for everybody. Each and every one of us is on a different life trajectory. Some of us, deep down inside, are not ready to get rid of our anxiety. Some of us are terrified of losing the anxious identity we've built over many, many years. Who would we be? I've been there, and it's terrifying.

The key here is that *you* must make a choice. Nothing on the outside, no book, person, blog, drug, or supplement, will end the anxiety *for* you. You and you alone will need to suit up and fight this to the end.

Of course, I can give you tips and tell you how I faced down anxiety and panic, but ultimately, you will need to find the tactics that work for you.

You are not alone in this journey, but you alone must make the choice to change the way you see life. I believe a lot of our anxieties are born from trauma and impressions we received when we were very young, possibly in utero. This is what we call "developmental trauma." These traumas could be overt experiences, neglect, or actions as subtle as "a look" from your father or mother. As adults who have experienced these traumas or received these impressions, we still see through the lens of fear, lack, worry, and stress they created. All this needs to be reframed and modified so you can see life just as it is, not as you think it is. And through that lens, life is a more peaceful place.

I believe my story and yours will intersect throughout this book. And in those aha! moments where we land on common ground, you will know your struggles are shared and others are on a very similar journey to yours. Even if I share a story or idea you do not fully relate to, I am certain you will benefit from reading it. Maybe not right now, but someday. Our stories are the same and different.

So whether you're challenged by general anxiety, full-blown panic attacks, or depersonalization (feeling detached from your body), it'll all be covered here. The key to this process is to jump in and lean forward. Anxiety will not just go away on its own. You need to be an active participant. I'll help show the path forward. Trust me. Trust yourself. Trust the process.

QUICK FIX

WE LIVE IN A TIME OF INSTANT GRATIFICATION. WE WANT CERTAINTY *NOW*. We want security *now*. We want money, happiness, peace, joy, and love *now*. And a lot of the time, we don't want to put in the work to get those things. The good news is the path to recovery I have set forth in this book is fairly simple. However, it is not easy or quick. It takes a lot of work.

Many, many years ago, when I wanted so badly for all the terror, pain, and self-judgment to just go away immediately, I reached for the quick fix of medication. And I did nothing else. I had just started college, I was very young and scared, and I didn't want to put in the work required to face my demons head-on.

Bottom line, quick fixes don't work. When I went off my medications in my early twenties, the anxiety eventually came roaring back because I hadn't done any of the hard work necessary to get to the root of these feelings. Conversely, when I faced whatever fear came up, rested in the fire, and listened intently, the fear eventually retreated, and I felt empowered. Moreover, my ability to face this monster got a little bit stronger each time I confronted it. I became more resilient. Most of the time, what comes easily in life doesn't last. What lasts doesn't come easily. Change *will* happen if you commit. But it requires showing up every day ready to face this challenge. *Every* day, without fail. It takes effort, and it takes time.

Once you commit to dealing with your stress and anxiety head-on, you've put many subtle processes into motion. And the universe is conspiring with you. The moment you committed and picked up this book, your internal systems began to churn and reorganize. Know that, subtly, this stuff is already working itself out inside you.

You are on a mission here. It's a mission that may take a bit of time, but I believe it's a mission you are built for and one that is very much worth accepting.

"BROKEN" TO OPEN

For decades, anxiety kept me imprisoned. I felt cut off from the world and everyone in it. I felt like I was the only one going through what I was going through. I was confused, I felt less-than, and I felt ashamed.

I kept everything to myself, locked up inside. That only made things worse. All these thoughts, insecurities, and fears had nowhere to go, so they bred with each other and created mutant thoughts that were worse than anything I could have predicted. I saw horrible visions of things I thought were about to happen—a massive car wreck, bodies flying, blood everywhere. It was devastating to my mental and physical states. I really thought I was going mad. When I looked in the mirror, I saw what everyone else saw: a calm and self-assured individual who was in great physical shape. But inside, it couldn't have been more different. I didn't know what was going on, and I didn't know what to do. This uncertainty about my well-being, my mental state, was feeding the monster.

When I finally did approach that psychiatrist in my early college years and he told me, very succinctly, that I suffered from something called "panic disorder," the brokenness I felt lifted a bit. Little did I know I was right at the beginning of a long journey of struggle, ups, downs, moments right in the middle, joy like I had never felt before, and unbelievably painful periods I thought would never end.

What I ultimately realized is I'm not broken. And neither are you. This is the hand I was dealt, and I had to deal with it.

Soon after college ended, when I went off of the meds, I leaned into more alternative methods, like meditation, conscious breathwork, and supplements. I'm not sure how exactly I stumbled on these options, but I will tell you I was drawn to them. I remember wandering into a record store in Georgetown, D.C. After having a conversation with an employee about anxiety, he steered me to the CD *Shamanic Dream* by Anugama and a pack of incense. So began my meditation practice. That simple interaction served me well and most likely changed the course of my life.

These alternative methods led me on a journey of inner exploration and deeply feeling emotional states I had never felt before—specifically, calm. I realized I could actually breathe a certain way and settle down my nervous system in a very short amount of time. That was huge. Slowly but surely, I owned my pain, and I opened up about it, first in therapy, then to close friends and loved ones. It was very frightening for me and a slow process because it went against everything I was feeling, which was tremendous doubt and fear of being judged. I was taking a risk.

I soon realized talking about my situation, trusting others, and learning opened up a new world for me. A world that wasn't so bad. I also realized many others were experiencing similar emotions. I was not alone. When I spoke about my pain very honestly, others felt free to reveal their vulnerabilities. This real-time loop of safety was something I had never experienced before. There was no longer this secret festering inside me, creating pain on top of the already existing pain. For the first time since anxiety entered my life, I realized I would be ok. It was freeing. I said to myself, "I can do this and, just maybe, beat this."

My struggles with anxiety forced me into self-discovery. I am pretty certain if I didn't have this challenge, I never would have begun this deep inner journey. The brokenness I felt turned into self-acceptance, self-realization, connection, openness, and a bit of peace. And, in turn, my creative life became deeper, richer, rawer, and more vulnerable.

I will say that now I am careful about how much I share, especially when going through a relapse (these do happen) of some sort. These periods can feel just as bad as the first time I experienced anxiety and panic. I also must be very gentle toward myself or run the risk of exacerbating the situation, perpetuating the story of fear, pain, and sadness. It's like the grooves on a vinyl record. The more you play that record, the deeper the grooves get. It's a fine balance between being vulnerable and open and protecting yourself when necessary.

Early on in my journey, sharing was imperative. But now, I have to be conscious not to use sharing as a crutch, leaning on others when I need to self-resource. I have to discover what that pain is trying to tell me on my own. At some point, you need to stop talking and start living—pushing yourself into situations that temporarily may feel quite painful or demoralizing. I know I am starting to sound like a masochist, but I can't tell you how important leaning into the uncertainty, the pain, the fear, and the panic was to taking my well-being to another level. Once I took that chance and everything turned out ok, I felt safe leaning further into the dark abyss.

There is nothing like the feeling of knowing you and you alone can face whatever life throws at you. Once you get to that place, so much of your anxiety falls away, and self-reliance takes its place.

HOW TO USE THIS BOOK

I AM NOT A DOCTOR, PSYCHOLOGIST, OR CELEBRITY.

However, I do believe I am an expert on anxiety and panic, as I've lived and suffered with both for over three decades. In that time, I have created my own simple tools, ideas, and philosophies that can help you face your anxiety head-on, just as I have mine.

I know there are hundreds if not thousands of books on the subject of anxiety, some clinical and boring, some overwhelming, and some simple and basic. And when you get right down to it, the concepts and tools are all the same. The tools that *really* work you can count on one hand. So I've tried to make this book simple. Simple concepts, simple ideas, simple practices. I know complexity breeds anxiety. My suggestion is you take from this book what works for you and toss the rest. You may even want to modify some things to fit your specific needs.

Change can be challenging. Hell, it's one of the things that creates anxiety. Everyone is different. What causes tremendous anxiety for one person may create euphoria for another. So, you may find that some of these concepts are easy to grasp, while you may struggle with others. Some of the material may be confronting. It may challenge the way you've thought about this topic for a long time. It's important to go at your own pace. Do what works for you. And when it comes to the stuff that is the *most* confronting for you, you should investigate *why* that is the case. I will tell you I am not here to coddle you. I am here to help you grow.

Because of my screenwriting background and my love for drama and tales and their powerful metaphors for the wild and incredible journeys we embark on, I've separated this book into three distinct sections based on the philosophies of storytelling.

This three-act structure is a narrative pattern that appears in most forms of drama, myth, religious ritual, and psychological development. It describes the typical adventure of the archetype known as The Hero, the person who goes out and achieves great deeds on behalf of the group, tribe, or civilization. The acts are as follows:

THE SETUP

In this section, our first "act," we set up the foundation and get you acquainted with the world and where we are headed. Here is where we take a breath, land, and settle in.

THE CONFRONTATION

In our second "act," we talk strategies and tactics and further build on the foundation we've set up. Here, you must look deep within in order to gather knowledge and tools to assist you on your journey. We must be present, be aware, and listen.

THE RESOLUTION

The third "act" is where we push ourselves beyond the realm of what we thought possible. We may need to completely let go of everything we've learned up to this point and let our souls guide us from here.

I've aligned these three stages of storytelling with the deceptively simple tenets in which this book is rooted—tenets that, once practiced, will take you down a path to clarity, self-love, peace, and self-confidence. Every teaching in this book boils down to these tenets:

Breathe

You must do it consciously, consistently, and deeply. This will bring you into presence.

Observe

You need to pay attention to and understand the data-flow in your mind, developing a keen awareness of your beliefs and thoughts in order to break your patterns. Ideally, you will go even deeper to understand where these were implanted—but you'll need to understand from a visceral, physical exploration, not from the mind. The mind tends to get in the way. What is your body telling you? This is a very non-judgmental exercise. Get quiet, and observe.

Let Go

Stop resisting. This, in my opinion, is the most important point.

You need to hone your ability to dance and *sit* with your deepest, darkest thoughts; sensations; emotions; and fears; moment to moment, over and over again. Everything you think you know about yourself may need to shift. If you do just this one thing, your life will change dramatically.

When I say "sit with it," that is exactly what I mean. Sit down, turn off all distractions, maybe close your eyes, and notice what comes up. No matter what it is that surfaces, stay with it. Observe it. Don't fidget, don't scratch the itch, don't do anything but watch your thoughts as you stay rooted in your body.

That's it. Every chapter, every concept, every word falls into one of these tenets.

There will be concepts, ideas, and theories repeated throughout this book. They will intertwine, amplify one another, and sometimes contradict each other, but again, it all comes back to the three tenets above: breathe, observe, let go.

If you get overwhelmed, confused, angry, or anxious while reading this book...

Breathe, and get present. Drop into your body. Feel it.

Ask yourself what you are feeling and believing in the present moment and why, and sit with whatever comes up.

Leave everything you *think* you know about anxiety behind, and charge ahead.

Let's do this. Inhale, hold, exhale. *Breathe*.

THE SETUP: Breathe

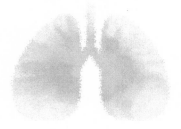

THERE IS NOTHING WRONG WITH YOU

I MET GURU SINGH, MY SIKH MENTOR, A DEAR FRIEND, AND AN ALL-AROUND beautiful person, during a time in my life when I was looking for something deeper and more mind-expanding than traditional yoga. Guru Singh says, "It's my deep belief that Kundalini yoga—the 'Yoga of Awareness'—is an access point to a sense of joy, ease, peace, calm, and completion."

Guru Singh's unique classes included extended philosophical teaching along with a yoga *kriya*, which is a set of physical movements paired with deliberate breathwork intended to uncoil Kundalini energy lying dormant at the bottom of the spine. This energy heals and blasts through emotional and physical blockages throughout the body. Guru Singh's classes led me to one-on-one sessions, where he would deliver measured and potent life advice, followed by Sahaj Shabd treatment sessions, where the Intention is to balance one's subtle energies through sound. I would lie on a bed cocooned in a blanket and surrounded by finely tuned speakers. My body would rumble for an hour or so, and I would feel completely refreshed and grounded at the end.

Guru Singh once told me that people with dyslexia, anxiety, depression, and certain mental illnesses are actually the ones who are well, and they are in touch with the rhythms and energies of life and the universe. He believes these people have an ultra-sensitivity to their environments—to people, animals, and life in general. They may have too much sensitivity, and that is why they tend to break down so easily. Society labels them wrongly, saying they have a "disorder," "illness," or "sickness" or they are "crazy."

Where one person may call an individual's terrifying emotional experience a psychotic episode, another may define it as a spiritual awakening. A few years back, I was really struggling and thought something was deeply wrong with me. Everything in my life, personally and professionally, felt like it had reached a breaking point. I thought I might be having a nervous breakdown. Instead of reaching out to a therapist, I felt called to contact a spiritual mentor. She was able to put things in perspective for me and soothe my concerns about losing my mind. What I learned was I was actually growing. That growth felt so unnatural to me; it felt utterly terrifying. The idea was if we can simply reframe these stigmas and cast away society's labels, understanding we just may have a superpower instead of an illness, healing has a head start.

This way of thinking is beautifully exemplified in a documentary called *CRAZYWISE*. In it, the filmmakers show how mental illness is treated in other areas of the world and, more importantly, how the views of some indigenous peoples contradict Western society's approach to those who are different (or "highly sensitive," as Guru Singh would say). The film explains how psychological crisis can be a doorway to positive transformation.

The two subjects of the film, who struggle with emotional issues that stem from childhood abuse and other traumas, have been victims of the devastating effects of over-medication and a society bent on fixing something that may not be broken, or, at the very least, attempting to fix something with the wrong tool. Over the course of the documentary, the two turn to kinder modalities, like meditation and spiritual training, that allow them to open the door to a richer and more natural recovery. Can we learn something about dealing with our own anxieties from this perspective? A resounding *yes*.

Of course, there are certain situations that require psychiatric interventions, and I don't want to minimize them. But in our Western society, we are quick to label people as "mentally ill" or "crazy" and point them to medication.

I struggled for years thinking I was broken. I believed only something "out there," outside of myself, could repair me. This was a very anxious and weak position for me to be in. But then I realized that, just maybe, there really wasn't anything wrong at all and that only my perception of things made me feel that way.

Roman emperor and Stoic philosopher Marcus Aurelius said, "Today I escaped from anxiety. Or no, I discarded it, because it was within me, in my own perceptions—not outside."[2]

I have stress, anxiety, and panic. Does that mean something is inherently wrong with me? No. Do I have a disorder? *No*.

I believe pharmaceutical companies want you to buy into that notion. They love labels and stigma because, you guessed it, they help them sell more drugs. Actually, the art of advertising is based on the simple concept that something is wrong with you or your life and this product ("our product") will correct that deficiency and make your life beautiful. Bullshit. It will give you *all* the answers until it doesn't. Then, they will pitch you another product. As long as you believe something is wrong with you, you are susceptible to others, to the marketplace, to your own skewed thoughts and beliefs. To anxiety.

You have a *challenge*. Acknowledging your ever-present anxiety could allow you to see life completely differently. To ultimately know yourself, others, and the universe more intimately than you ever would have without that challenge. This isn't denial. It's simply a matter of reframing. I know this may sound bizarre, but you could actually think of yourself as having a superpower: extra sensitivity.

Again, I'm not discounting individuals who clearly have a clinical problem. What I am saying is we are very quick to label individuals who struggle with what *appears* to be mental illness as broken or lost causes.

The medical model today treats symptoms, not their causes.

I can attest that this special power can be a godsend if you are a creative. Creativity and mental disturbances have historically been linked. Some people say this is a myth, but you cannot deny the numerous artists who suffered from anxiety, depression, or other mental illnesses. And it's clear most artists are highly sensitive and have a keen ability to see the world differently. I believe there is a bit of truth in this quote often attributed to Aristotle: "No great genius has ever existed without a strain of madness."

This high sensitivity, the ability to feel deeply and fully, allows you to be a more compassionate, loving, caring individual to others *and* to yourself. Deep down inside of you, at an atomic level, there is nothing wrong with you. Your mind is telling you lies, and you are complicit with your mind.

You run to the mind to escape feelings.

Know that you are not alone, you have the ability to get better, and you *already* have all the tools you need to get there. One foot in front of the other. Why create more stress for yourself?

I hope that is something you are willing to buy into.

HI, MY NAME IS ANXIETY

I AM VERY CAREFUL NOT TO PRESENT MYSELF AS A VICTIM TO MY FRIENDS, to my wife, or to myself.

I am very selective about the language I use when I speak about my anxious sensations and feelings. I am also selective about whom I speak with about these feelings. I am very careful not to create an identity around them.

Overall, I try my best to speak less. I find in doing so, what I do say is much more impactful.

Why?

According to a popular refrain often attributed to Gandhi:

> *Your beliefs become your thoughts.*
>
> *Your thoughts become your words.*
>
> *Your words become your actions.*

Your actions become your habits.

Your habits become your values.

Your values become your destiny.

A simple belief has the potential to shape and form your life. That is a pretty big deal, especially if that belief is negative and self-defeating. Even worse, this can be happening unconsciously. To be clear, I will use the word "unconscious" in this book when referring to feelings, memories, and deep-seated beliefs outside conscious awareness. This aligns with Sigmund Freud's psychoanalytic theory of personality.

Personally, I continue to reframe what is called in screenwriting circles my "backstory." In screenwriting, backstory is the character's major life moments that shape his or her beliefs, fears, motivations, and overall personality; for me, my backstory is the anxious identity that formed when I was very, very young and that I built up over the years.

Through my present actions and words and how I carry myself, I am able to reshape who I think I am into who I have always been at my core.

We need to recognize anxiety is not our identity, but we tend to confirm and embolden the idea that it is over and over. We tell ourselves and others, "I'm anxious." "I'm uneasy." "I'm scared." We need to stop empowering our anxiety with this language.

Instead of saying, "I'm anxious," we can say, "I am having anxious thoughts."

Instead of saying, "I'm uneasy," we can say, "I am having anxious sensations and feelings in my body."

Instead of saying, "I'm scared," we can say, "I am feeling scared."

After all, you wouldn't say, "I'm cancer," or "I'm irritable bowel syndrome," would you?

We have built up this idea about who we are through the way we talk about ourselves, and anxiety is a very big part of that. We start to believe our proclamations and then use confirmation bias to strengthen our position. Confirmation bias simply means that instead of looking at evidence on its own merits, we search for evidence that confirms what we already believe.

Through our language and bad habits, anxiety becomes who we believe we are at our core. We convince others that *we are anxiety.* We tell everyone. And it is hard to shake. Our language and beliefs become negative and unconscious, which feeds the monster.

Words and language are unbelievably powerful. Just a slight shift in usage can have a tremendous effect on your psyche and state of being.

Hi, I am *not* my anxiety.

FEAR IS A DEFENSE

THERE HAVE BEEN TIMES WHEN I SAT IN FRONT OF MY COMPUTER, STARING at a blank screen, about to dive into a new screenplay, wondering:

What the fuck am I doing?

No one will want to read this crap.

Who do I think I am?

This idea is crap.

I don't have the chops.

I haven't done enough research and planning.

I can't do this.

The fear these thoughts generate can be immobilizing. The strong urge rises in me to click over to the internet—to porn, to email—or just get up and leave my desk in order to distract myself.

That is exactly what the fear wants to accomplish. It arises as an attempt to protect you—your patterns, your belief system—to keep you stuck, "safe," by flooding your system with feelings of anxiety and dread. It's bizarre, I know, but this failsafe has been hard-wired into our systems from the days of the cavemen. The thing is, in 2022, the chances of you or your family not being able to eat if you don't go out and kill a large animal every day are very slim. Our nervous systems are running on very old software that is now corrupt. As the *Harvard Business Review* puts it, "You can take the person out of the Stone Age…but you can't take the Stone Age out of the person."[3]

Again, the fear instinct is meant as a protection, but it is anything but. In the modern day, fear attempts to protect you from perceived ridicule, embarrassment, and shame. So you see, fear can point you in the wrong direction. In doing so, it keeps you small—and scared.

Here's an interesting discovery of mine: the screenplay ideas and projects that terrified me most ended up being, in my opinion, my best work. They pushed me the most and helped me evolve as a writer. I believe this was the case because these particular stories required me to look at my own deep, dark emotional material and work with it. And then put it out into the world for everyone to see. I believe the best creative work comes from a profound personal connection to the material you are working on. This book, for instance, was a challenge for me. How much do I reveal about my journey, my life, my family? Well, a lot of it ended up on the page. And I am proud I didn't pull any punches. Because if I did, I don't think it would be as helpful. There is always resistance for me when I create. It's just part of the territory. What am I going to reveal to the world, and how will I be judged in the process? The irony in all of this is that when you enter a creative flow, anxiety is banished.

Your fear, if you flip what you think about it on its head, is valuable because it can be a signal, a signpost, as to where you should direct your attention, not what you should push away. My fear directed me exactly where I needed to go.

Of course, real danger must be avoided. But most of the time, there is no real danger. I am about to make an important phone call, not swim with great white sharks.

You must determine what is real—when you should trust the fear—and what is not—when you should lean into your circumstances. When the anxiety grabs hold of my chest and squeezes, when my breath shortens, when my mind's chatter starts, I look around and ask, "Am I in any *real* danger here?" It's an exercise in taking an honest inventory of your external and then internal worlds.

Byron Katie, speaker, author, and creator of a wonderful process called "The Work," outlines this precise method.[4]

1. Is my thought true? (Yes or no. If no, move to 3.)

2. Can I absolutely know it's true? (Yes or no.)

3. How do I react, what happens, when I *believe* that thought?

4. Who would I be *without* that thought?

The good news for us anxiety sufferers is that the majority of our fears, maybe even up to 97 percent, are *not* real. Researchers at Pennsylvania State University studied individuals over an extended period of time and found that 85 percent of what they worried about never happened. Moreover, the study found that 79 percent of the subjects felt they handled the 15 percent that *did* happen better than they thought they would and that they learned something valuable from the situation.[5] This means 97 percent of the time, there was nothing to be worried about. And that gives us a huge advantage! Most of the time, our minds are trying to protect us from things that are in no way dangerous. Most likely, when we experience fear, it is a False Event that Appears Real (FEAR).

When I apply these questions to my own anxieties, I usually quickly realize what I am feeling on the inside doesn't have anything to do with what is going on in the external world. It's my *interpretation* of that world. An interpretation that is very old and most likely born from the scars of a traumatic childhood.

I now often see fear as a sign that I should move forward, not seek shelter. That I am on to something. As crazy as it sounds, the more fear I feel, the more I am probably on the right track, moving toward eradicating the things that hold me back. Every time I hit a deeper layer, I am challenged even more. But I know it is a sign I am on the right path. It allows me to sit with, and then burn off, the underbrush—the deeper levels of pain and fear—and reintegrate with the parts of me that shut down and disappeared. I pause, breathe, face it, sit with it, experience it, and, most importantly, feel it—then watch it recede back to where it came from, leaving me to do my best work.

The more you do that, the less fear will rear its scary-seeming head.

FEAR IS TELLING YOU SOMETHING IS WRONG. BUT...

...IT MAY NOT BE THE *RIGHT* WRONG THING.

I used to have a constant ticker tape running through my head that screamed, "**BREAKING NEWS: SHIT'S ABOUT TO GO DOWN. TAKE COVER.**" And yes, it screamed in bold all caps. More often than not, my systems were in overdrive for no particular reason.

I know this because when it screamed, there was usually no threat at all. I'd be sitting in a movie theater with my wife, I'd be driving along the Pacific Coast Highway on a beautiful day listening to some great music, I'd be meditating. Absolutely no danger. In those moments, my inner turmoil overrode the natural events I was experiencing.

My feeling about fear now is that for people like myself—whose circuits are a bit crossed, who have been labeled in the past with some sort of anxiety challenge—when fear and dread strike, our minds are lying to us. There is *nothing* really wrong in those moments. What is really wrong, I am starting to realize, is our interpretations of what is going on. Interpretations cemented when we were very young.

Our job, over and over, is to tease out when The Fear is actually giving us some useful information. Like, "Hey, you may not want to drop your snowboard into this double-black-diamond ski slope during a whiteout," or "Don't take the larger dose of MDMA during your psychedelic therapy session because you may just flip out."

When The Fear crops up for me now, I ask myself, "Is this actually fear that needs to be addressed, or is it false fear that I need to just...allow?" I step outside of myself, just for a moment, to be more objective about the situation. I become the observer, the witness, just a bit removed from the melee. This takes practice and usually getting very still. Conscious breathwork or meditation will allow you to shift into a different, non-reactive perspective. More often than not, when The Fear crops up for me, I am reacting to a false alarm from the past. As soon as I bring awareness to this process, The Fear retreats. Maybe a little at first, but eventually, it completely vanishes.

The Fear is really telling me, more often than not, "I'm gonna keep challenging you until you realize I am a paper tiger. I am Oz behind the curtain."

I can't tell you how many times I've thought I had some sort of illness that was going to take me out and refused to investigate it on the internet. I just sat with it and let it move through my body, metabolize. Eventually, my mind dropped it. More importantly, my strong heart didn't explode, it kept on beating. My mind didn't short-circuit, and I lived to see (since I didn't lose my eyesight, as I had feared) many more days.

Of course, our deepest fears are born from our upbringings, all the environmental and genetic groundwork that set up our systems like this. Yes, those traumas play a role. Probably a big role. But none of our deepest fears line up with what is happening in the present moment. We are usually playing back old tapes that fuel fear, and we refuse to erase them.

You're ill. Get to the doctor before it's too late.

Your writing is shit. Give it up.

That's not what a real man would do.

Now when I listen to my tapes, I hear the words, feel them, and let them be there, knowing I have the choice to believe them or not. To act on them or just observe.

When we get down to it and simplify everything, it's just a deeply ingrained misperception. Incorrect meanings we give to The Fear. *None* of the outlandish things I have been overly anxious and fearful about have happened up to this point in my life. Maybe that is what's really wrong: we are empowering something, fear, that only exists because we give it life.

"FEAR IS EXCITEMENT WITHOUT BREATH"

THE TITLE OF THIS CHAPTER IS A POPULAR PHRASE ATTRIBUTED TO FRITZ Perls, who developed Gestalt therapy with his wife, Laura Perls.

Psychologically, fear and excitement are very similar and born from similar chemical processes in the brain. This similarity between these two emotions became very apparent to me in a place that at first struck me as very odd, the bedroom. I've noticed when I'm being intimate with my wife, I tend to feel fear first. Since I never felt safe when I was younger—safe to express my emotions, safe to feel vulnerable, safe to feel, always concerned about doing the *right* thing—I bring this stunted mindset into the bedroom.

I've heard that the bedroom is a microcosm for how you show up to everything in life. Makes sense to me! The act of making love, if intentional and truly loving, is extremely vulnerable. So when I get turned on and the well of excitement builds, I feel exposed, which leads to fear.

Not only that, but the chaos of my childhood, especially coming from the women in my house, was terrifying to me. My alcoholic mother's drunken episodes would include laughing, yelling, crying, and uncontrollable body movements. And my sister developed a very serious eating disorder and engaged in violent vomiting sessions. Consequently, at times, being sexual with a woman has felt threatening as I have misinterpreted bodily excitement and emotional states as something dangerous. Pleasure and ecstasy, from my view, are similarly highly chaotic and emotional. I feel excitement build inside me, I want to stay, it's all too much, I want to run, my wires get crossed, confusion sets in, I unconsciously take this as a threat, my breathing gets shallow, and the initial exalted feeling turns to fear. The repercussions of this wiring have shown up as early ejaculation, deep shame, and frustration.

On the other hand, I notice when I have a bit of control, slow everything down, make time for lovemaking, and am kind to myself, my body relaxes, and it is much more enjoyable. I'm now thirteen years into my marriage, and I still need to be on top of this recurring dynamic.

Ask yourself, "Am I scared or just super excited?" It really comes down to the meaning we give to the sensations coursing through our physical and mental bodies. The label we give these sensations takes us down one road and not the other.

When I'm fearful, I tend to breathe shallowly or hold my breath. That usually exacerbates the situation. If I breathe deeply, into my belly, slowly, consciously, that fear can miraculously turn to calm excitement. Like so many things I will mention in this book, a lot of your healing will come down to your perceptions of things, the meanings you give them, feeling the emotions born from these meanings in your body, and correct breath.

Since fear and excitement both activate the same part of the brain, the hypothalamus, and produce similar physical and chemical reactions—increased heart rate, increase in cortisol, preparation for action—distinguishing between a proper fear response and excitement can be challenging. The goal for us anxiety sufferers is to live more in the exaltation of excitement and less in the grip of fear. It's a small reframe. Maybe it's as simple as looking at fear as excitement.

FEAR OF FEAR

When I started college, my anxiety and panic kicked in hardest when I entered a classroom.

At first, I forced myself to stay using berating tactics like calling myself weak and a pussy or asking myself, "What would my father think if I ran out of here?" I white-knuckled it. It was extremely hard for me. As my world was coming apart, I maintained an assured and calm outer appearance. I did not want to appear weak to others, and I certainly didn't want to admit to myself I was struggling and needed help. I didn't want to fuel an unbelievably negative perception of myself. Unfortunately, my focus became my intense symptoms and feelings, my lack of self-worth, and my interpretations of all of it rather than the lessons that were supposed to help me become a well-rounded and informed adult.

One classroom was particularly challenging for me. I constantly felt trapped and on the verge of suffocation, especially if I was forced to sit in the center of the room. This was the birth of my fear of fear, which eventually became a phobia for me: phobophobia. And ultimately, it exacerbated my anxiety. It became less about the environment, students, teacher, or lessons and more about avoiding the tremendous fear I felt in that room. I didn't want to enter that particular classroom because of the dread it instilled in me. I didn't want to feel that fear that intensely ever again.

Let's say you attempt to start a business, creative project, or intimate relationship, and numerous uncomfortable feelings start to arise. More often than not, they swirl and build, creating additional feelings, emotions, and negative mind chatter that get locked into your nervous system.

Some of my mental tapes:

You shouldn't be feeling this way.

No one else feels this way.

You're a pussy.

You will never not *feel this way.*

These feelings will keep you small and unsuccessful in all areas of your life for the rest of your life.

These emotions and this self-talk can be exacerbated if any of those new business ideas, creative projects, or relationships turn out to be, in your eyes, your perception, failures, or your mind tells you a story about what you are feeling that allows you to remain blind and comfortably unhappy instead of one that may instill a bit of fear *but* pushes you to grow.

Fear builds and becomes the focus, the predominant feeling. This fear gets louder and more insidious, and you begin to forget what event, experience, or thought triggered it in the first place.

You don't want to experience this mind-bending fear ever again.

It is important to understand you've been training yourself to be this reactive individual for years, to be on guard, hyper-vigilant, a fear detective. It's primal, and your survival depended on it.

Eventually, my fear-triggering experiences—public speaking, intimacy, heights, confrontation, failure, success—move into the background, into the shadows, and what takes their place is the fear of this fear.

Basically, the fear that I will feel fear.

Franklin D. Roosevelt knew all about this. He alluded to it, paraphrasing Henry Thoreau, in his famous first inaugural address. "So, first of all, let me assert my firm belief that the only thing we have to fear is fear itself—nameless, unreasoning, unjustified terror which paralyzes needed efforts to convert retreat into advance."[6]

Although Roosevelt was addressing the nation's slow recovery from the Great Depression, it's hard to separate this sentiment from the fact that at the time, he was struggling with debilitating pain and paralysis from polio. He was talking about facing *his own* misfortune and fear of fear. And this appears to be a mantra reminding him to place fear only where it is necessary.

Fictional character Walter White from *Breaking Bad* didn't mince words when he spoke of his fears, "I have spent my whole life scared. Frightened of things that could happen; might happen; might not happen. Fifty years I've spent like that. Finding myself awake at 3 a.m. But you know what? I came to realize that fear is the worst of it, that's the real enemy. So, get up, get out in the real world, and you kick that bastard as hard as you can, right in the teeth."[7]

No matter how many times I faced a particular fear in the past, maybe even pushed through it successfully, when I find myself in similar circumstances, there is a feeling that I may not be able to handle the fear this time around. Once the snowball of self-loathing, fear, anxiety, and panic gets rolling in me, I need a strong tool to stop it.

Awareness. You need to understand the data flow in your mind, which is usually kicked off by something uncomfortable felt in the body, in order to break your patterns. Otherwise, you are on autopilot. Mindfulness and meditation are wonderful modalities that will allow you to discover what exactly is going on in your head. Once you are aware of your inner machinations—what you are believing that caused or triggered the fear—and not focusing on the fear or panic itself, the snowball begins to, very slowly, melt.

These fear mantras from hell lasted well after I received my undergraduate degree. Not only did I not want to feel that fear, I didn't want to hear those voices in my head again. Then, I would feel like crap because of what those voices were telling me and beat myself up for believing them. To be honest, I still hear the voices now, but they tend to be whispers, not screams.

Now, it's most likely you fear feeling fear—the anticipation of horror—and not the actual interaction, event, or experience. And that fear is nothing to be fearful about.

However, be careful. When things settle down and you start to feel peaceful, focused, or joyful, another strange fear may rear its ugly head.

THE FEAR OF...
NO ANXIETY

Here is the routine:

I've had an unbelievable day of writing. Stellar. The kind of flow state I pine for. I feel proud. The Southern California weather is what it is most of the time (gorgeous), my inbox is light, and everything is clicking, everything is in sync. My wife and I have a sexy date night planned...and then, there it is, a subtle tightness in my chest. Remember, the body is where it all begins. In his amazing book *The Body Keeps the Score: Brain, Mind, and Body in the Healing of Trauma,* Bessel van der Kolk explains, "For real change to take place, the body needs to learn that the danger has passed and to live in the reality of the present."[8]

And then questions begin to surface, not the good kind, that feed the fear, which blossoms into anxiety. It makes sense, right? Everything was going *too* well. The mind is a sneaky and insidious little bitch. When I am feeling no anxiety, that creates unease and, in turn, anxiety. Yes, you heard that right. It's kind of like those slow, chill moments in a thriller or horror movie. The calm before the storm. You know some shit is about to go down. Because deep down, it feels like the danger has not passed. Or if it has, only temporarily.

I've been suffering with anxiety for decades. Much less as of late, but it's certainly still there. That is what I know. Anxiety influences how I engage with many levels of life: my relationships, my family, my career, and certainly myself. Frequently, when I'm feeling anxious, I have to force myself to interact, force myself to be present, and force myself to stay when I want to leave or get away. A state of calm and happiness doesn't come naturally to me. I feel naked without anxiety. I created an identity out of it, remember?

When I don't feel the tentacles of anxiety, I feel so different, uncomfortably different. So I start to question, "What's going on? Aren't I supposed to feel anxious right now?" But I'm not. I actually feel good. Something must be wrong. What then transpires is a downward spiral right into the anxiety that didn't exist in the first place and I've tried so hard to avoid. Who am I without the nervousness, the pressure in my chest, the depersonalization, the demeaning and torturous voices in my head, the fear of imminent death?

We know sadness can trigger fear and anxiety, but joy can too. The wonderful book *Conscious Loving* by psychologists, authors, and body-intelligence pioneers Kathlyn and Gay Hendricks speaks of "upper limits." Gay says that when we get to a certain point of success or happiness in our life, we psychologically knock ourselves back down a few pegs. It's like we are so comfortable being stressed, anxious, and unhappy that joy feels strange. It's a similar concept to what I'm speaking about here.

When there is too much joy and excitement coursing through my system, too much feel-good energy, the warning signals start to flash. I'm at my limit, so I must put a quick and severe end to it. Individually, we have a certain amount of joy, pleasure, and peace that we will allow ourselves to experience. This limit could be set by things we've learned from our caregivers, peers, or society or derived from our self-imposed rules and regulations.

Once we hit that upper limit of ecstatic joy, something so foreign to us, we get scared, shut down, and run back to the safety of sadness, depression, anxiety, and fear. Because it feels comfortable. It's a contraction so ingrained in our bodies and individual psyches that it takes a lot of heavy lifting and awareness to break the pattern.

Notice when you start to feel peace, joy, confidence, or well-being in your life. What preceded it? How long did it last? What did you start telling yourself once you started to feel it? How soon did it disappear?

I started telling myself I didn't deserve to feel calm and peaceful. More specifically, I told myself a state of calm and peace would keep me oblivious to potential danger. So what did I do? I created a scenario, almost always unconsciously, some sort of brutal internal dialogue or external drama, that would put an end to those positive feelings. I needed to get back to what felt comfortable. This jolt of awareness of what I was doing shook things up for me big time. It made sense because I was so numb for so long.

You must nurture the deserved highs that come from hard work. Know that you have earned them. They are the direct result of your yeoman's work. When you aren't feeling fear, you are feeling joy, peace, and calm, which means you are aligned with your deepest self, beyond the traumas and childhood impressions. Those feelings are your human birthright. That's true human homeostasis. Don't question those ecstatic states or you may get answers that'll bring you right back to a place of uncertainty, confusion, and pain. You deserve every moment of the bliss you are feeling. Remember, no anxiety is a good thing. That's what we are shooting for here.

WTF?

I'm dying. No, you're not.

I'm going crazy. Nope.

I'm leaving my body. Maybe, but only temporarily.

I need to go to the hospital. Nuh-uh.

I need meds. No, you don't. Ok, maybe for a short period of time, but that's it.

Then WTF?

Welcome to my world. So many questions, and too few answers.

In a movie, usually toward the beginning, there are many questions posed, a lot of setups. This is to create mystery and uncertainty, engage the audience, lock them in, and knock them off balance. Great in a movie, but for everyday life, not so great.

The first thing I do when anxiety and panic strike is run to my mind, try to figure it all out. What I *should* do is breathe. On some level, anxiety is triggered by a feeling of being out of control, and I find if I take control of my breath, it ratchets me down just enough to gain a bit of control over my mental state. If I don't know what's causing all these strange sensations in my body or creating these crazy thoughts, thoughts I believe to be mine, it makes me feel more anxiety, and then still more anxiety. *What is happening to me, and why? Why me? WTF?!* See where the focus goes? These sorts of questions turn the heat way up—and not in a good way.

Asking the question, "What the fuck is wrong with me?" is so general, so scary in its own right. It has so much intense energy behind it. And it never led me to the answers I was looking for. It always created more anxiety. Because whatever you ask for, deeply believe, or focus on, you will receive. If you ask negative, frightening questions, you'll most likely get negative, frightening answers. And they have a tendency to spiral out of control, building and building to a very uncomfortable end point: an anxiety attack. Or at the very least, analysis paralysis.

Remember, your mind is trying to protect you from potential pain or hurt in the future, maybe because of some traumatic event you experienced in the past. So it appears your mind is lying to you. Your mind searches for the answer, the potential outcome, usually landing on a disastrous one, like cancer or severe mental illness. Your mind wants to prepare you for it.

The problem is that as anxiety sufferers, we *don't* trust ourselves. We really don't trust that our bodies and minds will work together to thwart the perceived attack, the illness, and get us out in one piece.

Over the years, I've learned I need to stop searching for answers, especially when I am in a state of distress. I used to search and search, mostly on the internet, for that article, book, workshop, YouTube video, podcast—that *answer*—to make it all clear.

I'm not saying some of these things aren't useful and won't help alleviate some of the pain. *But*…in my experience, general mental-health-related searches tend to exacerbate the problem.

That world out there, the internets, is populated by people that prey on your insecurities. I'm not saying this in some sort of conspiratorial way. Usually, the top links from anxiety searches are going to create more fear in your life, not less. All roads lead to cancer. Oddly, I actually find myself continuing to search endlessly *until* I find that cancer is a real possibility. It's like I want to validate my fears and end the search. There are so many different results, hundreds of millions, that you aren't able to process what's right for you. It always makes me feel *more* out of control. Moreover, the fact that you are searching means you've admitted to yourself something is wrong with you. That just feeds the anxiety monster even more.

What if you turned off your phone, stepped away from your computer, got still, ventured *inside*, and asked your own higher self quality questions? Like, "How could I be a better person than I was yesterday?" Or, "What would make today super fun and joyful?" You have the answers; you just don't trust yourself.

American religious leader Daya Mata discussed this in her book *Finding the Joy within You*. She said, "The Divine Voice within us will help us to solve all our problems. The voice of the conscience is a God-given instrument of divine guidance in every human being. But in many, it is not heard because over a period of one or countless lives they have refused to pay any attention to it. Consequently, that voice becomes silent, or very, very faint. But as an individual begins to put right behavior into action in his life, the inner whispers grow stronger again. Beyond the semi-intuitive conscience is pure intuition, the soul's direct perception of truth—the infallible Divine Voice."[9]

Stop constantly searching for external answers and listening to the monkey mind. Go deep instead, and discover the internal knowledge baked into your body, your DNA. It's always there.

Ask positive, life-affirming questions, and get quiet; otherwise, you are susceptible to the collective fear that is always waiting to rob you of your peace and sanity.

ANXIETY MONGERING

I REMEMBER A BILLBOARD THAT WENT UP NEAR MY HOME IN LOS ANGELES during the Obama years. "Friends Don't Let Friends Get Nuked. STOP OBAMA!"

Fear, uncertainty, and doubt, or "FUD," is an actual term used by Gene Amdahl, an American computer architect and high-tech entrepreneur, after his former company, IBM, launched a fear-mongering campaign against his new company. It is a method of creating distrust in a competitor's product or campaign developed in the marketing industry. It is now a tactic constantly used in politics, sales, and marketing to get people to spend money and help the fear economy.

Movies, television shows, and books can also be sneaky culprits of disinformation and some of the most powerful ways to persuade and influence people. Fear is being sold everywhere. Especially now, with a very large portion of the world plugged in 24/7, internet marketers funnel spam to your inbox and bury clickbait in every square inch of your screen. Moreover, misinformation can be weaponized and target an individual's psychological weak spots. Social media also feeds our anxiety, making us worry we aren't living well enough compared to the carefully curated images on Instagram and posed Facebook vacation albums.

Fear is used to get you to vote for a particular political figure or buy a new car, a security system, a sweet AR-15, or that awesome new prescription medication.

The advertising and marketing business mission: to sell you anything and everything by making you feel like shit, scared, less-than. You constantly hear that this or that "thing" will make you feel better. Fear sells.

In Mark Manson's article "How Your Insecurity Is Bought and Sold," he explains, "If you can tap into people's insecurities—if you can needle at their deepest feelings of inadequacy—then they will buy just about any damn thing you tell them to. This form of marketing became the blueprint of all future advertising."[10]

Fear and anxiety are deeply connected. So your anxiety, from a marketer's perspective, is good for them. They want to keep you anxious and fearful. They want you to continue to be dependent on medications that may make you feel a bit better but also may only serve as Band-Aids. Then, by design, you develop a fear of coming off of them.

In the *Atlantic* article "Legal Drug-Pushing: How Disease Mongers Keep Us All Doped Up," journalist and author John-Manuel Andriote states, "By manipulating our fear of suffering and death, big pharmaceutical companies are able to keep us coming back for expensive medications."[11]

David Ropeik, a Harvard instructor and author who studies risk perception and risk communication, said in an interview, "Pharma is hardly the only industry that sells products to help people protect their health that preys on people's worries about their health…Fear has been built into the advertising of any company that sells something that can help keep you safe."[12]

Be keenly aware of this. Fear is being manufactured all around you, on an everyday basis. You need to create a firewall against it. Best way to do that? Turn off the news and ads (if you can), and be mindful of social media usage.

It's hard to get people's attention with so many different ad streams bombarding the consumer nowadays. Loud, scary, and intense usually draws attention.

You know that because you have a knack for manufacturing your own loud and scary.

IMAGINATION CURSE

IMAGINATION CAN BE A WONDERFUL THING. WITHOUT IT, WE WOULDN'T have electricity, television, the internet, books, movies, or art. It can also be our enemy. As Seneca the Younger said, "We suffer more often in imagination than in reality."[13] Being a creative, I know this firsthand.

I sit in my office and conjure up all sorts of crazy and unique ideas for my projects: apocalyptic scenarios, serial killers, a story of a whip-smart eleven-year-old epileptic who finds a door to a magical world high up in his backyard oak tree during a massive thunderstorm. Anything can trigger these insights: a conversation, a news article, or something that pops up in my meditation. It's a real strength of mine. All artists have an incredibly strong imagination muscle.

I believe that, even if you are *not* an artist, most people are innately creative. The imaginations of non-artists are just not as trained as that of a person who hones it daily. This can potentially create an even bigger problem: if you aren't someone who intentionally hones your imagination, you may not be aware when it's running the show.

Here's what I'm getting at: you cannot just turn this tool off and move about the world. Not without some serious effort. My imagination—this wonderful tool that inspires me, that assists me in creating wonderful projects with deep and exciting stories, interesting characters, thrilling action, and drama—also causes me great pain.

I imagine awful situations, from my dog dying a horrible death that I have no power to stop to witnessing a car blazing through a red light and T-boning another car as I wait at an intersection or me uncontrollably picking up a knife in the kitchen and stabbing anyone nearby. These imaginings can happen in a split second while I'm moving through my day; sharp, quick, bloody, violent visions that make me question my sanity. These intense, imaginary episodes include everything from what will happen in the future to all the things I could have done in the past—better, sooner, and more of—that would have made my present life so much better.

My imagination, your imagination, takes me out of the present moment.

Getting lost in your imagination can be a wonderful thing. Like driving down an empty ocean highway, blasting your favorite tune. Windows down, ocean smell, endorphins begin to pump through your system. Beautiful images of your life-to-be dance across your mind screen. You move your body to the music, you smile, you laugh; life is good.

Then, on the other hand, you may get a call that a friend or family member has come down with an illness, hear on the news about someone who committed suicide or an individual who lost everything in a bad investment, or find out about someone going through a brutal divorce, and your mind (imagination) goes to work. The catastrophizing begins.

Will I get a horrible illness and die before I realize my dreams? Will my marriage fall apart? Will I lose everything I've worked so hard for? It's emphatic. It's endless.

You superimpose someone else's pain onto your life and then create all these horrible, imagined scenarios for yourself.

The fear and anxiety this creates can be unbearable.

The key is to recognize these patterns before it's too late. You do that by pausing, breathing, creating space and stillness, and asking questions. Be aware and present with your imagination. *Am I making shit up, or is this real?*

This beautiful, wonderful tool that helps me birth creative projects can also manufacture a life contained inside one of my creations: a giant haunted house. My imagination can leave me riddled with fear if awareness is not brought to the forefront.

Personally, I try to let my muse run wild when I am ferociously creating and grab the reins to quickly shut it down if it veers off the path.

All of it won't go away, and that's ok. There is a level of anxiety everyone must deal with at some point in their life.

MELLOW ANXIETY

PEOPLE WHO DON'T SUFFER WITH AN ANXIETY CHALLENGE STILL EXPERIENCE anxiety. Sometimes, they experience panic attacks. I see it and hear about it all the time, from family members, friends, even strangers. Many of these people, who are actually experiencing the normal vicissitudes of life, not a challenge, are so quick to run to a quick fix when they experience "basic" emotional pain. They pop pills, abuse alcohol, smoke weed, or drown out everything with busyness.

According to a 2018 American Psychiatric Association poll, anxiety reached epidemic proportions that year. Americans reported feeling more anxious across the five key areas of the poll: health, safety, finances, politics, and relationships.[14] Abuse of Xanax and Valium and benzo-diazepine overdoses are on the rise. Most of the people abusing these medications do not have a clinical anxiety issue. *You* may be one of those individuals.

We are all suffering from too much input, too much information, and too many choices and multitasking in a world that is increasingly spinning faster, fueled by the constant, mostly negative, stream of social media and news. When you couple this with not having enough processing power, it's a recipe for disaster.

I'm telling you this because regardless of how you address your challenge, you will experience some level of anxiety. So don't think this will all just go away when you understand the machinations of anxiety and start to practice with some powerful tools. Your challenge will lessen, sure. But it most likely won't disappear. You certainly will have a different relationship with it.

The key is to figure out what normal anxiety feels like for *you*. What is your baseline? Maybe that measurement will require you to be off medication if you are currently on it. Once you know that, it will change the game.

In my college years, once I realized I had this challenge and started taking meds, things felt kind of the same all the time. Very little up or down. And that didn't feel right for me. It did take the edge off things, but too much. Life was not meant to be experienced as a flat line, which is often the result of taking antidepressants.

Now, I am not talking about the equanimity that you can develop as a result of meditation or other spiritual practices. A state of feeling all emotions, positive and negative, fully, with awareness and ease. I'm talking about emotional numbing. Moreover, I felt I was poisoning my body, becoming dependent on substances, even though it was helping me somewhat emotionally.

Since I've been off meds for decades now, I can pinpoint fairly accurately what is normal for me and what is not. Since you have this challenge, you must be keenly aware of this marker, as normal anxiety can easily spill over into something *not* normal. Moreover, excessive anxiety will most likely continue to crawl back and test you over and over again.

Rule of thumb: is there an obvious stressor causing your current anxiety? The death of a pet or loved one, an exam, a date, a job interview? Did you just down way too much caffeine? Us anxiety-challenged people feel anxiety when there is no stressor, and we can feel uncomfortable for no apparent reason for long periods of time. The feelings tend to come out of nowhere, or, better, *seem* to come out of nowhere. For me, I try to get still and ask myself, "Is this normal, or are my mind and body going into overdrive for no apparent reason?" Try it. Your system, your body, is unbelievably intelligent.

Remember, anxiety is part of life. More and more people are experiencing it every day. Often, when one mental fire is extinguished, another smolders and comes to life. Let this sink in. It will be tremendously helpful to know the next time your heart beats faster and your palms start to sweat. It could all be…normal.

WHAC-A-MOLE

IF YOU ARE OLD ENOUGH, YOU WILL REMEMBER THIS GAME. IT'S A VERY simple game I used to play on the beach boardwalk when I was a kid. Simple to understand but not that easy to play. You have a mallet, and you must whack the moles that pop up out of the five different holes in the game unit. When you hit a mole, another one pops up very quickly. As the game progresses and you whack more moles, the moles speed up. Your eyes dart left and right, up and down as you swing the mallet faster and faster toward the gremlins popping out of the five holes. Maybe it's not a coincidence that decades later, I would discover this was very similar to how the anxious mind works.

The "moles" of the anxious mind usually take the forms of thought patterns fueled by beliefs born from traumas that turn into feelings, emotions, struggles, issues, anxiety, and panic. For myself, I struggle with health anxiety. This is the new term for hypochondriasis. I usually feel some sort of physical sensation in my body, and then, I start to run with it. *I haven't felt that before, what could it be?* I quickly put that thought to rest, but suddenly, another one pops up. *Oh no, now I feel it in my chest.* I say to myself, "Relax, we've seen this movie before." Ok, all cool. But then: *Could this be the early stages of a heart attack? I should go see a doctor, right? Oh shit, it will be embarrassing if he tells me it's all in my head, anxiety. I'd certainly feel like an asshole if that happened.* And on and on, the mind moles breed and overwhelm.

As soon as I ride it out, whatever the ridiculous thought is, whatever the concern, worry, or fear, there is a small gap of relief. I'm ok! Nothing happened. The sensations are gone. It was all in my head. Relief. Then *boom*, another mole. Another physical sensation or mental formation sends me back down the mole hole. That moment of relief creates a vacuum. My mind does not like to rest. No mind likes to rest. They need to find that next problem to fix. *What is it this time, mind?* Cancer, severe mental illness, or some other bizarre obsession.

As you play this frustrating game, those gaps get smaller and the mental formations get bigger. I've learned this isn't specific to health anxiety. Whatever your flavor of anxiety, this pattern will present itself. It's exhausting. With some courage and practice, you can recognize this repetitive pattern for what it really is: a mind projection wheel. Or, more crudely, a mind fuck.

Bayesian theorist E. T. Jaynes said this occurs when someone thinks the way they see the world reflects the way the world really is, going as far as assuming the real existence of imagined objects. Yes, your mind is— guess what? Lying to you. It has good intentions, but it is misguided. This is exacerbated by the fact that the mind is always trying to figure things out. It's constantly in motion. What if you were ok with *not* knowing the answers to anything in this moment?

Sometimes, all you need to break this pattern is awareness. Breathe, and slow the hell down. When you notice and see things for what they are, you don't need to whack the moles at all. You need to observe and demystify them.

Start playing now. But don't chase those moles.

PAPER TIGERS

When I was in elementary school, there was a classmate I didn't get along with. He was much bigger than me, and one day, we came to blows. I remember all the kids swarming to the baseball field to watch "the fight." I was terrified. What had I gotten myself into?

As this bully and I were surrounded by curious students, I sized him up, put up my dukes, and asked myself one last time, "What the hell have I gotten myself into?" About thirty seconds later, I slugged him in his left eye, hard. Soon after, it swelled up like a pomegranate and turned purple. He was done. We were done. The fight was over.

I was in shock. I think I looked at my fist in disbelief. *Did I just do that?* Then a sense of accomplishment washed over me. I had just beaten this guy's ass. In less than a minute. How cool was I?

I had this warped "idea" of who this bigger guy was and all the horrible things he could do to me. I made him out to be this tough guy umpteen times more capable than me with his physical body and his fists and made myself out to be the underdog with no chance in hell. I created this false narrative. The thing I feared, getting my ass kicked, was created by an imagination run amuck. Remember, over 90 percent of the time, the things we fear are not and never become real.

American scholar Joseph Campbell said, "The cave you fear to enter holds the treasure you seek." My interpretation? Face your fears because most of the time, you will realize there was nothing to fear in the first place. Our warped thoughts, beliefs, and emotions get in the way. And on the other side, your reward is self-confidence and an inner knowledge that you can and will enter many more caves with great success.

Entering that cave that day allowed me to prove to myself, or, better, to my mind, that my perception was wrong and I had the nuts, the skill, and the strength to take this Goliath down quickly. You and I are wired differently and more susceptible than most to what I refer to as "paper tigers."[15] Our false interpretations of others and situations often instill in us fear and the need to retreat.

Most bullies, like my a-hole former fellow student, fall into this category: people who appear strong, solid, and threatening but in reality are flimsy as paper and, most of the time, really scared themselves. These tigers can also take the shape of events and things. Moreover, when your mind is churning out a barrage of lies, fear, and deceit, it is bullying you. This bullying can take a toll. It can beat you into submission. Soon, you raise the white flag.

Ironically, from your mind's perspective, it's protecting you.

Every moment you can, pull back the curtain of your particular situation. Try to see the reality. I can tell you from numerous experiences that I've encountered very few real tigers on my journey.

When you step up to that perceived tiger and face it full on, you will most likely surprise and empower yourself. What you once thought impossible now moves to your can-do list. When you enter that cave fully, you are rewarded with resilience, courage, and confidence. Moreover, the result is usually something you could never have imagined.

So when you encounter a tiger you think is real, don't detach from the situation or yourself. Walk around to its side, and see that it's really only 0.004 inches thick. Fold it up, and get on with your life.

DISCONNECTION FROM LIFE

SLOWLY BUT SURELY, I PULLED AWAY FROM PEOPLE AND SITUATIONS IN MY life because of deep fear and insecurity, anticipated fear/anxiety, or just being pulled out of my routine. I believe many people who suffer from anxiety do the same thing. Sometimes, this happens unconsciously. I say, "No, I'm busy." Later, I realize I was avoiding something; my decision was made out of fear—fear of embarrassment, humiliation, falling apart, dying, whatever.

I would call myself more of an introvert. I recharge by being alone. I tend to get over-stimulated, so I try to manage that as well as I can. I spend a lot of time in my office, thinking, researching, handling business, and writing. Being a writer, solitude comes with the territory. It's necessary isolation. It's only me and the page, usually. This *feels* safe. And it is great I found something I love to do that aligns with who I am at my core. But there is a tipping point. A moment when cutting myself off from the world becomes detrimental to my growth and well-being.

Humans are social animals, and I am a human. So it would follow that too much time spent alone is not good for me. With practice, I've gotten a lot better. A few years back, I went on a snowboarding trip with a group of guys I had never met before. Initially, a good friend of mine was supposed to be on the trip, but he bailed at the last minute. I thought about it and then said to myself, "This will be good practice for me."

That trip checked every anxiety box.

- Strangers.

- Strange location.

- Out of my routine.

- Comparing myself to a bunch of dudes in all different areas— physicality, snowboarding ability, and career.

I needed to push myself. It was challenging, but I came out the other side with some really great memories, new friends, and the understanding that most of the time, my mind holds me back.

I remember during one of my first therapy sessions after moving to Los Angeles, I told my therapist, Dr. M., "I find my imaginative world more interesting than the real world."

Dr. M.'s response, "That's not a good thing."

I still find the need to push myself to go out, engage, network, meet new people, and interact with others. Over the years, I realized constant isolation only increased my anxiety. It gave me a false sense of security. It felt good in the moment, but in reality, it was undermining my ability to enjoy life fully. I may have felt safe, but my world was getting smaller and smaller. And when I did step out of the cave, the anxiety swelled. We are social beings and need interaction on a regular basis.

Solitude is wonderful, but it must be balanced with rich interactions with others and with nature.

I need to connect more with my wife for God's sake!

Ultimately, what will bring you joy, well-being, contentment, and love is connection. Separation breeds anxiety. Or, better, *perceived* separation. Not to get too esoteric here, but we are all connected to everything. When we run from our anxiety, we abandon ourselves. That feeling of abandonment strikes more fear in us.

And around and around we go.

Don't withdraw. Don't hide. Stand strong in the face of all of it. You will be rewarded with the life you are supposed to be living.

IT'S ALL IN YOUR HEAD...
AND THAT IS THE PROBLEM

I BELIEVE THE MAJORITY OF WHAT GOES ON IN OUR HEADS, ESPECIALLY for us anxiety sufferers, is false, made-up shit leaning mostly toward the negative. I've told you that already, right? A few times. I call this the 90/10 rule because multiple studies have found that, for people who suffer from anxiety, about 90 percent of anticipated fears turns out to be unfounded. Well, it's so damn important I think it's worth repeating over and over because we tend to quickly forget this truth and fall victim to the siren song of negativity.

Everything is self-contained. Your thoughts, your beliefs, your memories, your perceptions, your knowledge, and your experiences are all bouncing off one another in *your* head. So when you look at what is before you, your "reality," you fact-check it with all this mind junk floating around in your mind. Do you see how this can be problematic? A completely internal process that tends to refute what is actually happening right before you in the present moment.

I've come to this realization after studying some of the foremost thinkers, thought leaders, and spiritual teachers of our time. All of their teachings boil down to this one philosophy, which was really the basis of Buddha's teachings:

"The mind is everything. What you think you become."

British writer Alan Watts, known for interpreting and popularizing Buddhism for Western society, said:[16]

"All that you see out in front of you is how you feel inside your head."

Adyashanti, enlightened spiritual teacher and author from the San Francisco Bay Area, says:[17]

"Let go of all ideas and images in your mind, they come and go and aren't even generated by you. So why pay so much attention to your imagination when reality is for the realizing right now."

These snippets of wisdom all touch on the same concept: the mind is the thing that creates the most problems for us. It stands in our way.

As we walk through life, we mine the raw data from our life's experiences as we attempt to understand the reality before us.

Then, to determine what is actually the truth, what is false, if we are safe, etc., these experiences collude with memories, implanted beliefs from others, traumas, and all kinds of other fun stuff. We are asking the mind, the thing that started all the problems to begin with, to figure out what is real, what is harmful to us, and what is safe. We are not experiencing reality as it is. Moreover, if this present experience is anything like a previous experience that made us feel really uncomfortable, anxious, or fearful—a trauma—our mind draws on that old data to color the present experience with the same tainted brush.

A simple example: my wife may ask me to do something that I don't really want to do. This could be a very basic thing, like moving my phone off the kitchen counter. I react with a shitty tone, anger, a jumble of nonsensical words, and passive-aggressive behavior. My reaction to this request is much larger than the situation warrants. Most likely, I am reacting to an event from the past when my mother or father demanded something of me that I did not want to do. And there was most certainly an event even before that, when I was very, very young, where this initial corrupt software was uploaded. You can see how very hard it is to determine what is real. You are asking advice from what we call in the film business "an unreliable narrator." Usually, an untrustworthy storyteller, frequently a voice over, that forces the audience to question their believability.

It gives me anxiety just thinking about it. Obviously, that's my intention here. What I want to make you realize is that more often than not, you cannot engage with and be led by the stream of thoughts rolling through your mind. Many of those thoughts aren't even *your* thoughts. They have been implanted by caregivers, society, and trusted teachers. They are old tapes, or maybe digital files, that need to be erased.

You must first investigate, then stop these patterns in yourself or succumb to the "realness" of these imaginary movies you project out onto the world. I will say this again and again throughout this book because it is so damn important.

The mind is a terrible thing to *trust*. You thought I was going to say "waste," right? What is actually being wasted is all the time you spend engaging with the trash the mind produces.

I know this is a hard pill to swallow. Because the mind is *us*, *me*; it's who we are; it's the collection of everything we've learned, experienced, recorded; and it's the basis of all our decisions moving forward. It's our identity. Here's the thing: you are *not* your mind. This static in your head is conditioned. Most everything you believe was programmed before the age of seven. Another phrase of wisdom attributed to Aristotle is: "Give me a child until he is seven and I will show you the man." Those conditioned thoughts and beliefs, either born from trauma or modeled off our primary caregivers, are what we want to release just as quickly as they come into our field of consciousness.

As I said at the opening of this chapter, the *majority* of what goes on in your head is made up. So *all* thoughts are not false. That's right, I said it. But you know that. Adyashanti says that this concept, that thoughts are not the truth, is a bit like homeopathic medicine. It plants a small seed that eventually blossoms into a solid defense against our negative bias. It is not an absolute truth.

Since our minds are so geared toward negativity and worry, if you grab onto that concept—*all* thoughts are false—you sit up straight in your chair and really start to pay attention. And it gets you on the road to understanding. A better proclamation would be that *most* thoughts are false, worrisome, or anxiety provoking. If you actually start fact-checking your own thoughts, I guarantee you will come to the same conclusion. All thoughts are real, but they are not necessarily true.

Where we should end up is the ability to move away from the mind storm and drop into our gut—our heart-mind, the intelligence of our heart and body—to really know what's true. Then we begin to understand the conditioned thoughts, separate them off, and give space for something more real and truthful. Not absolute, but closer.

Deep breath. I know, it's a bit of a mind-bender, but you already know this. We just need to peel back the layers of uncertainty, self-doubt, and worry, get back to our core, and see things just the way they are. Because in that space of stillness and clarity, there is nothing to fear.

YOU ARE EXTRA SENSITIVE

So am I.

That's a good thing. Anxious people tend to be empathic, to feel the feelings and emotions of others and our environments deeply and intensely. This extra sensitivity allows you to be a more loving, caring, and compassionate individual to others *and* to yourself. I believe most creative individuals are also extra sensitive. I can speak to that firsthand. What makes a great artist is someone deeply in tune with humanity, the earth, and the universe. They can then take their observations; distill them; translate them into clear, unique, impactful stories and art; and gift them to the world. However, this sensitivity on steroids does come with some drawbacks. You may shy away from large, noisy crowds or events. You certainly will want to retreat and be alone. Often.

The good news: this ability to feel the emotional depths of others most certainly means we can tap into our own. Moreover, the ability for us to feel the "negative" feelings and emotions of fear, worry, anger, and sadness is directly related to our ability to feel excitement, contentment, and joy. It's like yin and yang. One cannot exist without the other. Have you ever seen someone cry deeply, and then minutes later, they can't stop laughing? These circuits are enmeshed.

I realized this firsthand when I started therapy. Initially, my pain came to the surface with a vengeance. All the stuff I had repressed and denied for many years—memories of my childhood, like watching my blasted-drunk, alcoholic mother stumbling around the kitchen trying to prepare a meal, like finding buckets of vomit underneath my bulimic sister's bed, or like reaching into her mouth to remove a handful of pills she took in an attempt to kill herself—made me realize there was a lot of crazy shit going on when I was younger, and it was not normal. This was hard to digest. This gave birth to fear and anxiety like I had never felt before.

Of course it did. I most likely disassociated from these traumatic events, temporarily detached from my body and mind, sealed a tight lid over all of it, and then turned my back on it. When I opened the lid to fully embrace the trauma and these feelings and feel them fully, they cleared out and allowed for some highs, and joy, at levels I didn't know existed. That took some serious courage.

The more you become "awake" to the inner workings of *you*, your sensitivities, the more you notice the darkness, your darkness, coming forth. Why? Because you've given it permission. The more you are able to feel, the more you will feel *all* of it. Self-exploration begets more and more feeling. And this can all be very confusing.

Remember, our high sensitivity allows us to feel everything intensely. So when multiple feelings and emotions are surging through us, sometimes, we just don't know what to do with it all. And that creates fear.

We know sadness can trigger anxiety, but intense joy and excitement can also trigger anxiety. This is actually called *pleasure anxiety*. We tell ourselves, "This feeling is too good, so something must be wrong." Most people who experience anxiety have been experiencing it for a long time, so the positive feelings of pleasure, joy, and excitement feel strange. Because of that, they feel scary. They are all just feelings. All extreme emotions involve intense energy coursing through our bodies, which us extra-sensitive people usually interpret the wrong way.

I want to make sure you are aware that going toward these awesome feelings, allowing them, which is definitely what you want to do, most likely will cause your anxiety to rise. That doesn't mean you are getting worse. It actually means you are getting better. Your ability to feel—all of it, in all your high-sensitivity-ness—is being strengthened. Just be aware of this. You are extra sensitive. Don't be scared. It's perfectly normal.

OPEN YOUR PRESENCE

WHEN YOU GET PRESENT, THE FUTURE AND PAST (THE BIGGEST FEAR AND anxiety generators) dissolve into the background, the mind quiets, and your heart begins to lead the way. The good news is the heart leads with feeling. The heart has its own mind, appropriately called the "heart mind." Some scientific research reveals the heart is thousands of times more powerful than the brain in how it communicates with and regulates the human body.

Aristotle believed the heart was the most important organ in the body. Through his biological studies, he came to understand certain animals could move and feel without the assistance of their brains. This led him to believe the brain may not be the driver of movement and feeling.

Aristotle also considered the heart to be the center of reason, thought, and emotion, senior to the brain in importance.

This aligns with the historical cardio-centric hypothesis. In a nutshell, this is the belief that the heart not only controls movement and feeling but sensation.

In an ideal world, the heart would be in the head and the brain would be in the chest. With that setup, the heart would always lead the way, and it would lead from the present moment. The more present you are, the less fear and worry can enter your mind space.

You don't have to be sitting on a meditation mat or in the middle of the woods to experience this. You can be standing in the middle of Times Square and still experience a deep presence. It's really about paying very close attention to what is right before you. And within you.

By training yourself to drop into this state more and more, you will not only feel less fear, anxiety, and worry, but you will also tap into the powerful intuitive centers of the mind.

There have been numerous studies that prove this idea. Sara Lazar, a neuroscientist in the Psychiatry Department of Massachusetts General Hospital and assistant professor at Harvard Medical School, discovered that not only does meditation reduce stress, but it may also change your brain for the better by increasing gray matter. This has the profound effect of creating new neural pathways, which in turn can significantly reduce negative emotions.

The Stoic Seneca the Younger demanded presence: "Two elements must therefore be rooted out once for all—the fear of future suffering, and the recollection of past suffering; since the latter no longer concerns me, and the former concerns me not yet."[18]

Be grateful for the moments you are in and appreciate them, moment to moment. Your state of mind will greatly benefit from it.

DON'T WANT IT TO BE
ANY DIFFERENT

Too often, we chant the mantra, "One day, when I get that job, that perfect partner, that house, that piece of jewelry, that fill-in-the-blank, when all anxiety and stress disappears, I'll be content." This means you are not content in the present moment, not allowing the present moment to be. This means you are resisting what is—life. This is one of the core tenets of this book: resistance creates suffering.

We know how this story ends: you get that thing, and you feel great, content, for about thirty seconds, and then you zero in on that "other" thing you don't have. More resistance, more emotional pain, and more anxiety.

A wonderful exercise is to frequently ask, "Where am I arguing and fighting with life? Is it with my feelings? My life situation? Is it something I don't have and think will make me happy when I have it?" It's not the direct external experience that creates the pain and anxiety, it is the resistance to the experience that creates the emotional pain. I know it sounds counterintuitive, but as soon as you stop *wanting* your experience to be different, your experience *becomes* different.

Adyashanti says, "All spiritual practices that are worth doing are practices that either help us to see through whatever we're believing in the moment, or they help us let go of our resistance to what is happening."[19]

What is cool is that if you *really* get still—breathe, listen, feel, drop into the way things are and your perceived uncomfortable situation—truths will be revealed within that pain, truths that have been buried underneath layer after layer of conditioning. These truths may be as simple as, "When I lean into my fears and anxieties, force myself to stay when I want to run, eventually I experience silence and peace like I've never felt before."

Now, this isn't an easy practice, and it may take a few days, weeks, months, years, or possibly longer to refine. I'd be lying if I said otherwise. But do it, and you will reap the benefits.

Non-resistance doesn't mean give up, become a doormat, or surrender to physical or mental abuse. It means to let go of outcome, to let go of wanting the world to engage with you differently, to let go of the torment you are feeling inside, to let go of wanting any of it to be any different from what you are experiencing in the present moment. *And* at the same time, it means to take steps to bring more peace into your life as you let go of the outcome, moment to moment.

This was always a hard concept for me to grasp.

I liken it to a sneaky move in my jiu-jitsu practice where you move your torso and head backward to evade an incoming punch or weapon, and at the same time, your foot or hand moves forward to strike the attacker. You are giving way, letting go, and aggressively moving forward and striking your attacker at the same time. You can live in both of these worlds, non-resistance and attacking life, simultaneously.

As much as I don't want to write this chapter, I choose to plow forward in the face of all the bullshit stories I tell myself. Because I know each keystroke will bring me closer to the outcome: a completed book I am proud of. And whatever the result is in this present moment—great writing, or dreck—I am ok with it. In that ok-ness, not expecting a certain outcome, I'm free.

And in that freedom, really great writing ultimately does happen.

This will take practice, and you may have to read this chapter over and over again to get this concept to sink in, but trust me, it will.

Don't fight what is right in front of you. Allow *now*.

BREATHE, ALLOW, INVESTIGATE

ONE DAY, WHILE I WAS WORKING FROM MY HOME OFFICE, I WAS INCREDI-BLY anxious and on the verge of a massive panic attack. I sat down in a chair and began to breathe very deeply. At the same time, I took in my surroundings. It was all very intentional. I took in the grass and the trees outside my window. Then I zeroed in on the physical feelings in my body, like the surface I was sitting on, a breeze across my skin, the thumping of my heart, and the uncomfortable tightness in my chest. I was in this strange place of experiencing tremendous fear and, at the same time, feeling all would be ok. I let it be. Then, something happened that really surprised me. I shifted into a state of bliss.

Up to that point, I had never experienced a complete 180 like this, such a quick shift from terror to peace. I took deeper and deeper breaths, and as I did, this new feeling intensified. It felt so amazingly good. Maybe *too* good.

The three most important things you can do for yourself when in the grip of anxiety? Number one: breathe. You knew that was coming, right? I know it sounds basic, but when we become tense, we stop breathing properly. We breathe shallowly. This sometimes just goes on for brief moments, but other times, we stop breathing altogether. That lack of breath only makes things worse.

Most of the time, even when we are not tense, we are breathing much more shallowly than we should. This can happen while experiencing exalted joy *or* fear. I frequently monitor my breath, and it's interesting to see when it becomes shallow. It can happen when I stare at a huge to-do list, when I hear the sound of an ambulance or fire engine, when I watch a tense or frightening movie, when I practice jiu-jitsu, or when I make love with my wife.

Once you check it out, I bet there will be numerous instances when you think you are relaxed, but your breath pattern is telling another story. I bet your breaths are pretty lame and probably don't reach beyond the top of your diaphragm. You need to deepen them, study them, and feel them first before a more automatic practice evolves and becomes second nature. This is a very intentional practice.

Place your hand on your lower abdomen, and fill your hand with breath over and over. Pay attention to your breath. Focus on the air going in and out of your nose or mouth. Again, this may all seem counterintuitive or even impossible. If your mind is racing, heart is beating fast, and palms are sweaty, how do you sit with all those intense feelings and breathe properly?

Start with ten breaths deep into your belly. Breathe in through the nose, pause for a few moments, then exhale through the mouth. Pay attention to the out breath. Make it longer than the in breath. Repeat.

What you will find is focusing on your belly and breath will cause your overwhelming thoughts to drop away. As this happens, your body will relax, and a sense of peace and calm will take over. It's quite magical what a simple breathing technique can accomplish. If your anxiety is at peak levels, this practice will be challenging, and it may take a bit more time for your system to settle down. Don't worry. You can do it.

This leads us to number two: *allow*. You allow everything and anything that is happening to you: the thoughts, the compulsions, the sensations, all of it. Observe it. Allow it. We usually fight what we are feeling and deny it. That only makes it louder. What we resist persists.

Know that you are not in danger.

That day in my office, when things shifted and I was feeling so amazing, I didn't allow. I stopped all those pleasurable feelings soon after they started. Why? The intense joy I was feeling, just like fear, was too much for my system to handle.

Allow all the discomfort, whether it's coming from joy or pain. Trust me, I know how bad it gets. Just remember how strong and resilient this is ultimately making your nervous system.

This is Olympic-level training here.

You are rewiring your neurological system.

Breathe deeply and consistently, and allow everything without editing. Be curious. Know that you are feeling anxiety. Label it.

Every now and then, when I'm feeling brave, I'll ask for *more*—more mind chatter, a more intense heartbeat. More of whatever is feeling so uncomfortable.

I know this seems odd, but it short-circuits the process. Here I am, completely full of all these immensely uncomfortable feelings and sensations, and I'm asking for more. It tricks the mind. You are essentially leaning into fear and anxiety, staying with them, and proving to your body and mind that you can handle them.

The key is you need to be fully authentic when you ask for more of the uncomfortable feelings. You cannot fake it. You are so acutely aware of what is going on in your body and that your mind is lying that you are daring your mind to give you all it's got. Be brave. Go for it.

If you stick with it, you will ride the fear wave, it will crest, and then you will experience an amazing release of energy that you've probably needed for a long time. I've witnessed this firsthand numerous times. Fear subsides and calm, even bliss, replaces it.

The army retreats, the dust settles, and you feel like yourself again. This *will* happen if you let it. The intensity of anxiety, the electric jolt of panic, will work its way through and out of your system. Let it wash over you.

Through breath, feeling the sensations in your body, and allowing what is, you transmute, like ice to water, all this nastiness. In the process, you learn something about yourself. This comes with number three: *investigation*.

When you are in the throes of, well, let's just call it "temporary insanity," you need to bring yourself back to a point where you can make sense of what is happening to you. What is your body trying to tell you? It has a story, so investigate. Ask questions. "Were the thoughts going on in my head actually true? Do they match reality? What am I feeling in my body now as opposed to then? Is there tightness, tingling, soreness, a release? Does my body have something to tell me?" Breathe, allow, and investigate. Repeat.

If you are lucky, the investigation is where you are gifted a little tidbit of information and insight. It could be as simple as, "You made it through," "You did it," "You survived," "You faced down the lion," and in the process, you emboldened yourself, if only just a little. Next time, it won't be as bad. Out of everything else in this book, this chapter holds the simple keys to surviving the onslaught of anxiety.

Breathe. Again, it's simple but not easy. It's the one thing I can tell you is most often done wrong by individuals who have anxiety challenges. You must learn how to do it right—from fast, shallow chest breathing to slow, deep, conscious belly breathing.

Allow. No matter what the fuck is happening, you need to stay with the pain, the nausea, the urge to bolt, the feeling you are actually coming apart at the seams, the feeling a breakdown is imminent, or, God forbid, the feeling of joy. *Stay.* This was the hardest one for me. And you'll succumb over and over. Until you don't. Sometimes, you'll need to bail, and that's ok. There is a point where it *is* too much and going further could retraumatize your system. You'll know what that point is. Trust your body.

Once things start to settle down, you can *investigate* a bit. Find out where, specifically, the tension is being held. And if you continue your deep breaths as you shine a light on these unsettled parts of you, you may just get some key intel as to what this anxiety is all about.

I will tell you something, and this is something I'm still trying to get my head around (no pun intended): the body has all the answers. It will honestly tell you what's up, unlike the mind. It may be a subtle pain, a vibration, a racing heart, a shift in temperature, a tingling, a fullness. These are clues. You must get quiet and present and make sure you listen and observe closely. If you do, like a flower blooming, insights and information will come bubbling up from within.

NEWBORN STEPS

When I started training in Ketsugo jiu-jitsu, I quickly realized its unintended and unexpected benefits. The reason I searched out martial arts in the first place was to develop more confidence and feel more self-assured, not only in threatening situations but in everyday life. Jiu-jitsu helped me with this, and it also gave me lessons I could apply to my anxiety. One of these lessons was the process of taking things slowly.

"Slow is smooth, smooth is fast" is a saying you'll hear frequently in the martial arts world. As a general Ketsugo training practice, we move our bodies much slower than we would in a real combat situation. When you slow down and really tune in to your body, you notice inefficiencies, gaps, and other lapses in movement that can be worked on and improved and then sped up when necessary.

Another wonderful benefit of moving slowly is everything in your body becomes extra sensitive, especially your skin, which allows you to, when seriously threatened and in the midst of a violent attack, predict every move of your attacker. Obviously, this is something that needs to be practiced and developed. Repetition is key.

To practice this martial art quickly would seriously injure all involved. It *must* be practiced slowly and smoothly. I've jabbed a fellow training partner in the eye or otherwise slightly injured them more than a few times because my moves were too fast and I didn't have complete control over my body. I anticipated the partner/attacker coming at me and tensed up. I felt a twinge of anxiety, got all up in my head, and as soon as they moved, I jolted into action, usually too quickly. In turn, my neck has been tweaked because a training partner, in defense of my attack, was moving too fast or jerky.

I believe these and other accidents and injuries happen when we come at life too quick—from the head, not from the deeply felt instincts of the body. Moreover, when the head gets involved, we try to do too much at once. We get overwhelmed, which is shorthand for thinking about too many things at once.

When I get anxious and overwhelmed, I want to speed up. I want to do a million things at once. I'm trying to drown out all the negative feelings with busyness, and at the same time, I'm thinking that the faster I move, the more quickly I'll get out of the hell I'm experiencing. All of this is the exact opposite of what would actually benefit me most.

Just take it slow.

There is a wonderful book called *Bird by Bird* that talks about this process in relation to writing.

The author, Anne Lamott, talks about putting aside the idea of a finished book, screenplay, or whatever the final product may be. It's best to think about the next line, the next chapter, and, ultimately, what is right in front of you.

She says, "I go back to trying to breathe, slowly and calmly, and I finally notice the one-inch picture frame that I put on my desk to remind me of short assignments. It reminds me that all I have to do is to write down as much as I can see through a one-inch picture frame. This is all I have to bite off for the time being."[20]

I utilize this philosophy in my screenwriting. If I were to look at the entire pie, all the machinations involved with a screenplay—the characters, the plot, the escalations, the structure, the massive effort it takes to get from "Fade In" to "Fade Out"—at once, I would never be able to begin.

There is no need to rush this process or overthink it. Breathe; take small, manageable steps; and move slowly. Let it sink in, see what concepts you are attracted to, and practice diligently and slowly.

Chinese philosopher Laozi once observed, "A journey of a thousand miles starts with one step."[21]

I had a lot of fear when I entered the jiu-jitsu dojo. So many thoughts were running through my head: "I'll suck at this," "I'm gonna get my ass kicked." But I kept at it. I made progress, slowly. Now I feel competent and ready for a challenge. I know fear will still crop up as I learn. When it does, I'll take it one small, slow step at a time.

Remember, there is no quick fix to this anxiety bullshit. You must step up and face it every day, every moment, and slowly destroy it.

Be patient, be kind to yourself, and keep showing up.

MENTAL JIU-JITSU

1. Breathe.

2. Get out of your head.

3. Be extra sensitive to your surroundings and your physical body's place in them.

4. Be soft, smooth.

5. Go slow.

6. Flow.

7. Create.

You've heard a lot of these recommendations from me throughout this book, right?

Well, in this instance, I'm not speaking about anxiety training. These are teachings related to jiu-jitsu training, specifically Peter Freedman's Ketsugo jiu-jitsu, a style I've been practicing for six years now and love.

Freedman says, "In reality, our system has the same basic foundations as other traditional systems of Ju Jutsu. We just have a unique way of teaching it…The goal is to teach the student the ability to react creatively instead of thinking."[22]

After my wife and I were suddenly jumped while on a walk, my desire to learn self-defense became real and immediate. When someone places a gun to your head and tells you if you move, you will be killed, shit gets real—fast. I didn't panic in this situation. I went on autopilot. I actually became very calm, measured. And ultimately, we walked away from the situation unscathed. This is the way your primal system is supposed to work and will work when necessary.

Afterward, I was not ok emotionally. I began to question what I did right, what I did wrong, and what I should do next. I believe I was in a subtle state of shock. Here, my fear center was acting inappropriately.

There was certainly "a deer in headlights" reaction in the moment. If this situation had escalated, I'm not sure I would have known what to do or if I could have protected my wife and myself.

Because of this, I began to search out a self-defense style that would allow me to hone my offensive physical and emotional skills in the face of real and immediate danger.

What I was looking for in a martial art was something practical that wouldn't require years and years of training. I also didn't want to be beaten down physically and emotionally as a way of learning.

My classes take place in a park with no special attire (*gi*). They're very informal. The style, the practice, however, is beautiful, brutal, devastating, and deadly.

"Jū" can be translated to mean "gentle, soft, supple, flexible, pliable, or yielding." "Jutsu" can be translated to mean "art" or "technique" and represents manipulating the opponent's force against himself rather than confronting him with one's own force.

The tenets of this style, and I am sure other styles of martial arts—to let go of the mind chatter, breathe, feel your body deeply, and move slowly—are great wisdoms we can utilize to combat not only real, physical foes but, more importantly, our internal anxieties also.

After all, true martial arts are not just about self-defense, fighting, and killing. They are about a way of life that emphasizes well-being and improving physically, mentally, emotionally, and spiritually.

I now find that my practice beautifully aligns with and supports how I face my fears and challenges every day.

GET OUT OF
YOUR HEAD

As a screenwriter, my job is to get words on a page that lead to interesting characters, an engaging story, and an experience. Hopefully, an entertaining experience. I've been doing it for years. I'm a pro. But I still catch myself questioning the words I'm writing. "It's ok, but ok won't cut it. You know, this is actually probably shit. It's not making sense. Maybe to you, but no one else will understand it. Why am I talking to myself?" Now, I could indulge this inner critic—let it lead me down a path of frustration, anger, and despair—*or* I could just watch it, wave to it, smile, give it the finger, and let it go.

As I have said over and over, most of the pain and suffering we deal with in life are generated by our minds. It's not the events in our lives, it's how we interpret and react to them. The brain is a wonderful organ and absolutely necessary. It can also create intense misery for us—correction, it most likely *will* create misery for us.

It has been said that Einstein used to obsessively pour out his thoughts onto paper. He did this so he could use his mind for the important stuff, like changing the world with his theories, *not* remembering, forecasting, regretting, fearing, or worrying.

If you are constantly drowning in the torrent of your mind stream, then doubt, misery, and anguish creep in through the gaps.

How do you counter this bad habit? Change your state of mind! Better, get out of your mind. Do something physical every day. Take a walk. Take a run. Pull the blood and energy from the mind into your muscles and organs.

Seneca the Younger stated that, "We must give our minds relaxation: they will arise from rest better and more vigorous. Just as we should not impose commands on fertile lands—for uninterrupted fertility will quickly drain them—so constant toil will break down the impulses of our minds."[23]

Walking meditations are great. Walk into your yard barefoot and feel the earth beneath your feet. Really feel it. Ground yourself. When I walk my dog, Stella, near our house, as I take in the Pacific Ocean, I frequently pay attention to my feet as they hit the ground. Then, I feel my calves, my thighs, and so on. I try to inhabit my body.

Swim or take a bath. Immersing yourself in water is incredibly grounding and healing. Watch a hilarious movie or comedian. Laughter, especially uncontrollable belly laughs, will heal you at your core. Blast music and dance by yourself. Get into your body. Dropping into your physical body, even for a brief moment, can work wonders. *Shake* your body and limbs for five minutes straight—this one is great. Jump on a rebounder (mini trampoline) for five minutes. Have some great sex.

Do anything that helps you get out of that damn head. *Anything*.

Mystic, guru, Indian godman, and leader of the Rajneesh movement Osho, also known as Bhagwan Shree Rajneesh, has a wonderful guided dynamic meditation. It is an hour-long process involving intense breathing, screaming, shaking, catharsis, mantra chanting, silence, and, finally, celebration. It's specifically designed to get you out of your head and into your body, where shit you don't need can be released. You can find it here: https://www.youtube.com/watch?v=XOIYdmQ7kUw.

Leave the head and enter the body.

Engage in a ten-minute Wim Hof breathing technique. Wim, a Dutch extreme athlete, is also known as the Iceman. He has created an intentional power-breathing process that energizes the body and clears the mind, which creates space for more focus, creativity, and stress reduction. During this practice, you alternate between thirty to forty power breaths, breathing in and out deeply, followed by extended breath holds. Frequently, this brings on feelings of hyperventilation and lightheadedness, and if you stay with it, these feelings will transform into euphoria. I do this every morning, and it flushes my system and lights up my body while calming my entire nervous system. It's amazing and settles the mind instantly.

One of my favorites when meditating is to focus on each and every part of my body, from my toes to my crown. In doing so, I can feel where stress, anxiety, and pain live and then focus intently on releasing them. Usually, that is exactly what happens: they dissolve.

Move from the head, the mind, and into the body regularly, if only for a few minutes.

SHAKE UP
YOUR ROUTINE

BACK IN 2017, I WENT ON A TRIP TO EUROPE. MY WIFE AND I HAD BEEN talking about a trip for years—actually, almost a decade—and we just would not pull the trigger, which is strange because we didn't have children, we worked from home, and we really didn't have a good excuse. Nevertheless, we made up a few. We were busy and couldn't find that perfect timeframe that would suit us both. We couldn't leave the animals in the care of a pet sitter for that long.

We originally wanted to go to Italy and Greece since we each hailed from one of those countries. We thought it would be cool to go back to our roots. Then, we rationalized we couldn't fit those two amazing countries into one trip. I now think that was the main thing holding us back: trying to do and see too much at once. Eventually, my wife recommended a slightly scaled-back option: to strictly visit Paris and Rome. I said, "Let's do it." Since Paris was our original honeymoon pick, we thought we'd go there and put off Greece for a later trip.

Leading up to the trip, there were myriad things that instilled a low level of anxiety in me:

- How will my anxiety play out overseas?

- Language barriers

- Different currencies

- Different foods

- Lack of exercise

- Lack of writing/creative process

- Transportation/getting around

- Personal safety

- Accommodation stress

- Will I get to see and do all the things I want to?

- Fear of missing out

- Guilt for having fun

- Guilt for *not* having fun

Moreover, I hadn't been to Europe since the '70s, on a trip to Greece with my family. I had never been to France or Italy at all.

I was at the tail end of an intense, anxiety-riddled year and a half, and I really wanted to be more grounded before I took the 6,500-mile trek. Well, that wasn't going to be the case.

First stop, Paris: the City of Light. My anxiety grew. However, my wife and I jumped in full on. We did everything: Notre Dame, the Eiffel Tower,

Versailles, a candlelit dinner on a Seine riverboat, the Crazy Horse Cabaret, markets, restaurants, and massages.

I didn't work out, I ate everything, I indulged, I was a bit mischievous, and I played! At the same time, my anxiety lessened.

After four days, it was on to Rome. Wow, Rome. No words. The Colosseum blew my mind. The Pantheon, Sistine Chapel, and St. Peter's Basilica were not far behind.

Witnessing and soaking up the art and architecture of painters, sculptors, and architects in both of these cities was exactly what I needed. It showed me art comes in many shapes and sizes and dedication and honesty to the craft produce the most awesome results. The Trevi Fountain in Rome took over thirty years to complete!

Some of these artists proved the impossible because they didn't know they couldn't, many times to the detriment of their physical and emotional well-beings. Michelangelo was tough to be around, a loner, and married to his art. He also lived an extremely modest life, even though he was extremely wealthy. I was able to draw from the lessons of these amazing artists with the hope of incorporating them into my own process.

I also couldn't deny the hypocrisy of the Catholic Church. Rome has nine hundred churches. Nine hundred! Every hundred feet, there was a church that would blow your mind more than the last. It's hard to explain the beauty without actually seeing it. And underneath, you have darkness—and scandal after scandal. Not to mention the Ancient Romans were brutal people. Incest, torture, death as a sport. Literally every one of the seven deadly sins was practiced on a regular basis. While touring the Colosseum, where attractions involved fights to the death, I was made aware that many of the stones from there were used to build St. Peter's, the largest church in the world. The irony is hard to fathom. This reminded me of how intertwined polar opposites are and that only by knowing one end of the spectrum can you know the other: beauty/ugliness, light/dark, hate/love, panic-anxiety/calm, fear/trust.

As we got deeper into the trip, my anxiety eased even more. I didn't write, and I didn't feel guilty about it. I didn't respond to many emails, and I pretty much stayed off social media. I did whatever the hell I wanted. That amounted to sucking up the European culture of two amazing cities in a big way. I realized I was a voracious explorer, maybe to a fault. I wanted to see everything. My wife had to keep up with my rapid pace. I had *so* much energy. I realized I am not meant to sit behind a desk and be apart from people, at least not for long stretches at a time, which, as a writer, is what I do on a regular basis. When I was exploring, I was in my element. If I was learning in the process, which I was, all the better.

Very little anxiety entered my space. I believe this is because the whole trip felt like play. I felt like a little boy again. I had fun. And I did my best to suck up all the positive, creative energy that off-gasses from this part of the world. Witnessing and soaking up the art and architecture of painters, sculptors, and architects was exactly what I needed.

This trip inspired a lust in me to travel more, see more, learn more, and know that I was not alone in the trials and tribulations faced on the artist's path, the human path. I was out of my element and *not* stuck in the daily grind. The different locales and uncertainty of the day created a wonderful energy that inspired humor, sexual polarity, and deep love.

One of the biggest problems with anxiety sufferers is we do the same things over and over every day. This is by design. We have a routine we set up that we think will keep us calm. And it doesn't! Even though we may be suffering from keeping ourselves small or lacking spontaneity, it's nothing like the anxiety we believe we will experience if we don't have a routine in place. It's understandable, as change can be incredibly anxiety provoking. That's why you probably don't shake things up.

Certainty and routine are your safety blankets. They are also dull, boring, and soul-sucking. Keeping your routine the same will allow the existing anxiety to fester. And remember, routine creates certainty, but most of the time, it is an illusion of certainty.

Understandably, you must have a daily framework that allows you to do your best work, but it cannot be at the expense of living your best life.

When I returned home after a quick twelve days, I became sad. The euphoria of the trip slowly wore off, and I had a bit of withdrawal. What gave me solace was knowing these ecstatic feelings live inside of me. I don't need to be standing in the Colosseum to feel empowered, resting on top of the Eiffel Tower to feel joyful, drinking a glass of wonderful Italian wine at a small Italian bistro to feel romantic, or cruising the Seine to feel contentment and deep love toward my wife. I can be looking at a flower, staring at the ocean, holding my wife's hand, or taking deep breaths while sitting in silence with my eyes closed.

I feel proud of myself for how I arranged and planned this journey, and how I fully engaged with it. The trip I had resisted so much at first slowly morphed into the most mind- and soul-expanding, anxiety-*reducing* thing I had done in years. I will repeat: the anxiety was quelled, big time. I felt a huge shift. The thing that inspired unease and anxiety within me—this trip, the unknown—became the key to unlocking some of my most profound and enjoyable moments and, in turn, positive emotions.

I hope you are grasping all of this because as I've said before, I am not a superhero. We all have the same tools to work with. This means you do too. Shaking up your routine or travel doesn't have to be a two-week, international trip. It can be spending the day over at a friend's house, a trip to the grocery store, an overnight excursion, or, for some people, a walk from the front of the house to the back. Take a chance now! Shake it up! Maybe in small ways at first. Your mind and body will reward you for it.

BE NICE TO YOUR FUCKING SELF

ANXIETY *LOVES* WHEN YOU BEAT YOURSELF UP. LOVES IT. THRIVES ON IT.

My process usually goes like this:

1. I feel like shit.

2. I get anxious.

3. I judge myself for feeling anxious. And for feeling like shit.
   This results in feeling *more* anxious, shameful, judgmental, and
   like shit.

4. Repeat.

During this insane process, I am certain I am weak; I am less-than; I am a
pussy, a loser, stupid, a fraud, etc. Because if I wasn't any of those things,
I'd be able to snap out of this anxious misery instantly. Or better yet, I
wouldn't be feeling any of these things in the first place.

Bullshit.

You feel overwhelmed, sad, anxious, and/or depressed. In short, you feel like shit. You give yourself shit for feeling like shit. You feel doubly shitty. As if it wasn't bad enough just to feel shitty, you will now feel shitty for feeling shitty. Maybe, just maybe, you'll feel shitty for feeling shitty for feeling shitty. And down the rabbit hole you go.

It's a vicious circle, what wonderful Buddhist meditation teacher and author Tara Brach labels as "the second arrow," or coming down on yourself for feeling like crap. Not only the second arrow, but the third, fourth, and fifth come flying your way.

As if it's not enough to go through the pain and suffering of anxiety and all its physical and emotional symptoms as-is, we need to pile judgment and additional pummeling on top of it. I have been brutal to myself, analyzing and grading every single thing I do. It's either a success or a failure, nothing in between. Many times, I see my successes as lukewarm, as not up to snuff, or, even worse, as failures. As you can see here, I judge what I do and how I perform, not who I am.

I hope when you read this you can see how ludicrous this process is. It just doesn't make sense. The logic is if I am incredibly hard on myself, I will snap myself out of my misery. And because this reaction occurs so naturally, we just don't realize it.

Since we are with ourselves 24/7, and it's the most important relationship we have in life, the kinder and gentler you are when interacting with *you*, the better. You wouldn't treat anyone else in your life the way you treat yourself.

Plato said, "There is nothing worse than self-deception."[24]

We go to great lengths to create elaborate stories we tell ourselves in an effort to keep from moving forward, taking chances. They include berating ourselves and generally being total assholes.

Seneca the Younger said, "Wherever there is a human being there is the opportunity for a kindness."[25]

I believe this quote could first be directed toward ourselves.

Celebrate the little wins, forgive yourself for missteps, failures, or things you've done that lack integrity. Learn from them. Soothe yourself. Humor *really* helps. Laugh at yourself, at the absurdity of it all.

I find just talking to myself, giving myself simple reminders of the good I strive for in life, the people I have helped, and the integrity at the core of my being from which all my actions spring, puts me in a pretty amazing space. Try it for a few minutes, and then build on it.

LAUGH AT YOUR ANXIOUS SELF

THIS IS THE STUPIDEST SHIT I'VE EVER SEEN. I CROSSED MY ARMS OVER MY BODY and sank into my BackJack folding chair as I watched a group of grown men force themselves to laugh at nothing. The group's facilitator introduced the exercise with a simple promise: "Even if you start with a forced laugh, you soon won't be able to stop yourself from laughing *for real.*" It seemed I was the only one struggling with the exercise. The majority of the other men in the group were chuckling or laughing in some way. One guy was outright guffawing. But I couldn't bring myself to join them.

I don't know whether it was the foreignness of it or my own doubts and insecurities—was I doing it right? Is there a right way to force laughter?— or whether it was my fears—fear about what it meant that the other men could access laughter so much easier than I could. Whatever the reason, I was struggling. *Wow, it's really hard for me to laugh*, I thought. *I stuff it down just like all the uncomfortable emotions and feelings I have.*

In the life of the anxiety challenged, everything, and I mean everything, is digested through a serious lens. Part of that, for me, was growing up way too fast with too much responsibility. Of course, everything felt like life and death when my dad left town and told me to take care of my alcoholic mother. I was a child for Christ's sake. Now, as an adult, I still find myself drawn to the more intense things in life, whether it's music, movies, relationships, etc. Even if I may not particularly enjoy the intense moment, it feels normal and natural to me. Light and funny is, for lack of a better word, boring.

But humor and laughter is so good for the heart, the body, and the mind. The bottom line is laughter is a salve for anxiety. You really can't experience both anxiety and amusement at the same time. Hell, you can laugh at your anxiety and the challenges it brings. Not in a demeaning way, but a soft approach that finds the humor in the absurdity of it. So start watching more comedy and definitely stay away from the news, a.k.a. fear porn.

Full-on belly laughs are the target.

BUILD YOUR
WAR CHEST...A TEAM

You don't have to struggle alone. You need go-to people in your life as well as systems that can be pillars of strength when you feel unstable. My team looks like this:

- A psychotherapist specializing in childhood trauma and anxiety.

- My wife.

- A support group of like-minded people. I have a men's group I check in with regularly as well as a creative group of writers I meet with weekly.

- Significant others and loved ones I trust.

- My dog and cat.

My support groups are wonderful because they make me aware of my blind spots. I get honest, sometimes uncomfortable feedback as to where I may be getting in my own way. I am held accountable.

Most importantly, you *must* have some sort of "break in case of emergency" plan: a specific friend or individual—a lifeline—you can call at a moment's notice.

I know that reaching out for help can be a bit unnerving. Emotions like shame and embarrassment can rush to the surface. You may feel you don't want to burden anyone. You need to move past that. Vulnerability is key here and will actually assist you in purging your anxiety.

If you are uncomfortable reaching out to someone you know well at first, research therapists specializing in anxiety. There are also many free resources, so lack of funds is not a good excuse for why you are not building your team.

But remember, you must be careful not to use others as a crutch, leaning on them when you may need to self-resource and dive more into the pain.

With all that said, the most important (and often overlooked) individual on your team is *you.*

And within you is your *inner team,* which includes your inner allies and nemeses. These are subpersonalities, like your inner critic, your warrior, your bully, your rebel, and your saboteur.

Italian psychologist Roberto Assagioli, who developed a form of therapy called psychosynthesis, discussed our fragmented personalities. "We are not unified," he wrote. "We often *feel* that we are, because we do not have many bodies and many limbs, and because one hand doesn't usually hit the other. But, metaphorically, that is exactly what does happen within us. Several subpersonalities are continually scuffling: impulses, desires, principles, aspirations are engaged in an unceasing struggle."[26]

Clinical psychologist Michael R. Kandle supports this theory, saying that every sub-personality serves a unique purpose in our lives, purposes that often conflict with one another.

You need to make sure you and your inner team are not holding you back. Make sure your team members want to be on your team.

How do you get *you*, your inner team, on board? This could be as simple as having some inner dialogue when you are present and calm. Alternatively, you could engage in a deeper, more elaborate practice, like a guided cognitive-reframing process done with a skilled therapist.

Externally, everyone around you could be supporting you, guiding you, and providing you all the tools you need to pull yourself out of a life of anxiety, despair, and hopelessness, but if *you* aren't on board, if *you* are fighting against them, if *you* aren't willing to do the hard work, none of it will matter. Moreover, these external team members may resent you for it.

Build a team to support you, inside and out, and then be a team leader.

SIGNIFICANT SUFFERER

I'VE BEEN MARRIED FOR THIRTEEN YEARS NOW TO AN AMAZING WOMAN who deeply loves and cares about me. My wife was really the first woman to whom I was able to completely and fully admit my anxiety struggles. It certainly didn't happen all at once. I needed to build trust. Lots of trust. Then I had to be vulnerable, something I still struggle with every single day.

When I get vulnerable, every bone in my body says, "No, don't do that, don't say that, pain ahead." This is because I wasn't allowed to be vulnerable when I was a child. Emotions were not valued.

In those moments when I reject vulnerability, I push on. But I know the pain I will feel holding on to all this will be much worse than the short-term anxiety, embarrassment, and shame I may experience from embracing vulnerability. This rejection may even create other illnesses within me.

I love author Brené Brown's idea that we tend to reject vulnerability in ourselves and consider it a sign of weakness, but we tend to applaud vulnerability in others as an example of courage.

The insanity of this thought/feeling process is what I love, as it very quickly shows us just how absurd and skewed our mind patterns can be. Of course, it doesn't make sense, but it happens. Why do we do this? Well, insecurities within an anxious person can bring forth situations where they exalt others and hold them in high regard while beating themselves up in order to keep the anxiety in place.

I've come to realize that all the energy I used to keep my fears and my pain bottled up only created a shitload more anxiety.

If you are in a loving relationship with someone you trust and you have not revealed your anxiety challenges to them, you must sit your partner down and tell them what is going on for you, within you. If you don't, you will only create disconnection and pain for both you and your partner. If I am in pain and my wife has no idea why, it creates pain within her. She may start to second-guess what's going on, thinking she may be the cause of my pain, adding to the pain she already feels from watching me suffer.

I'd go as far as to say you will not be able to wrangle this anxiety beast to the ground unless you share your deepest fears with your wife, husband, girlfriend, or boyfriend. Besides, they know something's up. Others will know too. You can only mask this monster for so long. Your keeping the lid on all of this will only exacerbate the situation and cause the bottled up emotions to come out sideways, through anger, through avoidance, through withdrawal, and in the bedroom.

Vulnerability in all areas of your relationship is a wonderful thing. So why not share this part of you that takes up so much space? It's not easy and it does take time, but if that person truly loves you, your vulnerability will only deepen their love for you. If they *do* freak out, shame you, or ultimately leave you, you shouldn't have been with them in the first place.

BE STILL

If I could recommend the one practice that has changed my life the most, it would be putting the brakes on and becoming very quiet. Even just for a few moments.

When I wandered into that Georgetown record store, fresh out of college, I discovered a remedy to many of my ails. It was not a panacea, but it made me understand I alone could, if I chose, explore the depths of my mind and come out the other end a much calmer, clearer, less reactive human being.

That day in that record store, I discovered Anugama's *Shamanic Dream*, a CD with beautiful, calming music on it. That music allowed me to get out of my head and settle my nervous system, which then allowed me to still my mind. I never would have been able to do so on my own at that point.

Now, you probably think I'm talking strictly about meditation when I mention being still, and on some level, I am. But you don't have to have your eyes closed and be on a cushion, in a Zendo, or in a cave to become still.

Meditating on a cushion in a room so quiet you can hear a pin drop is fantastic, *but* you need to be able to take your practice, the discipline, into the real world and real life situations to put it to the test. Or, as someone once told me, *if you think your spiritual practice is strong, spend some time with your family.* Of course, it requires practice to reach that level of equanimity.

Most of us probably spend about forty minutes a day max in proper meditation. That leaves a whopping fifteen hours and twenty minutes of waking life left that we must show up to with calm and peace.

You can start right now by closing your eyes and taking three long, measured breaths. You can do this wherever you are. Become intently aware of what is going on in your body. Study your breath, where your skin touches the floor or the ground, or any other sensations. Don't worry if you are doing stillness right. What you think is an unbelievably crappy practice just may provide you with the best results and vice versa. Just do it. It's working.

One thing I've learned from meditating for decades is that it may feel like absolutely nothing is happening while you are doing it. Nevertheless, the cumulative benefits, which include better overall health, increased creativity, and heightened intuition, are undeniable.

Sometimes, we just don't know how things are moving, percolating, and shifting within us and the effects of it all. As you know, our perceptions of others and ourselves are skewed. Slow down, and listen. Carve out a bit of time every day to shut off the outside world. My entire daily practice is based on this. I start every day getting still and quiet. A mini mind-purge.

This will allow you to, very quickly, practice the main tenets of this book:

- Watch your *breath.*

- *Observe* your mind chatter, your *thoughts* and *beliefs.*

- *Let* it all *go.*

And feel really good, solid, as a result.

DON'T LOOK AWAY, GET CURIOUS

When I get emotionally triggered, locked into negative thought patterns, the fear and anxiety cycle starts. My first knee-jerk reaction is to try and make it all go away. *Why is this happening to me right now?* My mind is out of control, flooded with thoughts and images of dread, worry, and terror. *Shit. I'm falling apart. I need something or someone to grab onto. I'm going to turn my back, run, and find solace.*

In reality, I am running *away* from solace. And so are you. I'll put it another way: you are running toward short-term solace and long-term pain. This is akin to an alcoholic having a drink to alleviate stress or a workaholic taking on more responsibilities and tasks. It feels good in the moment, but as the pattern continues, it usually wreaks havoc in your life on many levels.

If you sit with the trigger and its aftermath, develop a curiosity about it, really observe it, engage with it, and feel it, you will short-circuit the process.

I'm sure you've watched horror movies before. You may squirm, your heart rate rises, and you watch the screen through the fingers of your cupped hands. But you don't run. You are *curious* about what is about to happen. So you endure. And then, after, there is usually relief and even laughter. A release.

What about a roller coaster ride? Same thing. Anticipation, sweaty palms, butterflies, fear, speed, hands in the air, eyes closed, eyes open, ups, downs, relief, laughter, and, finally, peaceful exhaustion.

Understandably, you know the outcome, but this illustrates the ridiculousness of it all. Even when the outcome is certain, that you will be ok, your mind ravages you with conflicting thoughts and emotions. This is evidence of how deeply ingrained and primal our negative patterns are. And the only way to purge those little bastards is to first recognize that they are actually happening. You need to become *aware*.

So, you must take your hands off your eyes and observe. What's going on inside you, physically and emotionally, when your switch gets flipped? Dig deep. Start asking questions, empowering questions. *How interesting that when A happens (externally), then B happens (internally)? Man, I remember when I was little, a similar thing used to happen.* And don't judge any of it.

Then let it work through your system without a need to know why.

Because every time you don't allow what's happening, what you are experiencing, you are setting yourself up to be challenged once again.

This practice is by no means easy. You will continually screw up, and that's ok. Just keep showing up, being curious. This simple little action will create the small gap necessary to break this insidious pattern.

THROW IN THE TOWEL

FOR SO LONG, I'VE STRUGGLED WITH THE IDEA OF THE PERFECT CAREER, the perfect accolades, validation, attention, the perfect home, the perfect income, the perfect relationship/marriage, the perfect diet, the perfect meditation, the perfect therapist, the perfect spiritual life. I want it all and for all of it to be perfect. Because if all of these things are perfect, it will make *me* perfect. It's exhausting and fuels stress and anxiety. The irony is that, even though the intention is pure—to be complete, whole, fulfilled—we are actually creating more stress and anxiety in our lives. Not to mention perfection doesn't exist!

I feel a constant striving in my life, a desire for forward movement and growth, a fear of missing out, of someone getting a leg up on me, of my life passing me by. Some of this is good. It's motivational. But a lot of it feeds the anxiety monster. Paradoxically, many times, in those moments of grasping, my life *is* passing me by.

Wouldn't it make sense to stop fighting for your life all the time? To stop, if only for a moment, the comparing, monitoring, checking, listing, and scheduling? Remember, us anxiety sufferers want to control everything because we think if we do, we can ward off the anxiety. However, it only gets stronger.

Find your surrender sweet spot.

Give in. In moments. Maybe days or weeks. Maybe when you find yourself completely overwhelmed, just stop, take the day off. Do nothing. Counterintuitive? Frightening? Sure. But you can do it. And you will be better for it.

Or maybe ask for help. We can't do this all on our own. Take some damn things off your plate! You'll find that so many things you have on your to-do list don't need to get done immediately, or even at all. Delegate. Virtual assistants can be a godsend.

Stop striving. Stop competing. Stop comparing. Stop resisting. Completely. You just may be surprised that when you really boil down your life to the most important things, these behaviors likely aren't on your list.

I find this works best for me when I incorporate "nothing breaks" throughout the day. And I do mean *nothing*. I am not trying to get anywhere or solve anything. I am not even trying to do nothing. I just take in the moment and see what comes up. I'll sit in a comfortable chair in my office or home and just stare out the window. I'll ask myself, "How can I be doing *less* right now?"

If you're like me, stress and anxiety tend to speed you up. So initially, this practice, *really* stopping and shutting everything down, might be very confronting because it is so foreign to you.

You need a complete and definitive break every once in a while. Probably at least once a day. Yes, this will bring up anxiety. Good. You will start asking bizarre questions. "Am I just wasting time?" "Will I lose everything I've practiced so hard for?" "Will I fall back into old patterns?" "Will I be considered lazy?" "Will I miss out on something?" What's interesting is when I get really still, physically and mentally, it's easy to see myself trying to *do* something in these quiet moments. *Is this the perfect posture? Should I close my eyes? Should I focus on something in particular? How should I breathe? Should I ignore thoughts?* Ahh, the mind. Most of the time, it is not your friend. When it has nothing to do, it gets pissed. It can get loud and very mean.

You need moments of nothing to balance all the noise, busyness, and chaos. You need to give up on fighting every single thing in your life.

The cool thing is that you are getting your body and mind used to doing absolutely nothing. This will get easier as your practice deepens.

Try this out: when you finish this chapter, go find a quiet place to sit, and just be. Do nothing. Five minutes is plenty. You may get quiet enough to allow peace, calm, and something really magical to break through. Giving up never felt so good.

A GIFT, NOT A BURDEN

WHEN I WAS IN MY EARLY TWENTIES AND IN THE GRIP OF PANIC AND ANXIety, I was terrified. I felt like a small boat being tossed about in a massive ocean storm. There was nothing to grab hold of. I felt as though this dark, heavy weight would follow me around for the rest of my life, if I survived.

When anxiety first starts to invade our lives, we all tend to have the same reaction. We ask, "Why?" Then we resist, run, hide, and beat ourselves up for feeling this way, reacting this way. Because we have no knowledge of exactly what is going on inside of us nor the tools to quell the upsurge of emotions and sensations, the anxiety skyrockets.

As life went on and I gained more knowledge, understanding, and clarity around my anxiety, I saw the gifts birthed from this challenge. I became very curious as to how my brain, and, in turn, my mind, worked. And eventually, I developed a sense of compassion for myself and others who struggle. This was a huge reframe and inspired me to explore a creative life.

I believe my emotional struggles influenced my choice to become a writer and filmmaker. Not only did I develop a curiosity around what made me tick, I wanted to know more about others, why humans do what they do.

I wanted to share interesting stories of struggle and overcoming adversity. I also believe my anxious mind pushed me to be more vulnerable. I have come a long way in this area, but this is something I continue to battle with and work on every day. Because emotions, positive and negative, feel terribly overwhelming! I don't know what to do with them, so the last thing I want to do is share them. My knee-jerk reaction is to recoil and put a lid on them, and this only makes the anxiety worse.

Who knows where I would be if I didn't have this challenge. One possibility is that I would skip along the surface of life, completely oblivious to the richness and depth of my inner world. Of life. This may be the biggest gift my challenge has afforded me.

Those dark places I've visited were terrifying in the moment, but as I look back, I'm able to learn from these harrowing journeys, extract some real wisdom, and understand who I am at my core. As an artist, I believe you *must* go to those places. It's where the real rewards are unearthed and brings creative work a richness sourced from the depths of humanity. Look at your life. I would bet the challenges, the adversity, are the things that have truly defined and shaped you, made you a three-dimensional person.

I'd like to pause and reflect on all the wonderful things anxiety and panic have provided me. This is by no means an exhaustive list:

- A search for meaning.

- Deep inner exploration.

- Deeper compassion toward myself and others.

- Deeper compassion toward life, pets, and the earth.

- Humility.

- Deeper understanding of what makes me tick and why.

- Confidence in the face of debilitating fears or circumstances.

- Realization of my true emotional, mental, and physical strength.

- Understanding the unbelievable malleability and trainability of the brain and mind.

- All the wonderful self-care practices I use daily.

- Slowly but surely, a larger sense of humor.

- The ability to *feel* life deeply, all the ups and downs. And knowing I'll be ok.

- Vulnerability.

- The ability to inhabit and feel my body, the emotions and sensations that course through it, like never before.

- The inspiration for some wonderful creative projects.

- The ability to be in service to others who are in emotional pain.

- A portfolio of projects born from my curiosity of the mind, humankind, and the choices people make.

- This book, the instruction manual I wish I had when I was younger, where I can now share all my experiences with others and hopefully *help* in some small way.

Thank you, anxiety.

Some people say ignorance is bliss. Maybe in the short term. But the long term? Nope. My anxiety has become one of my greatest spiritual teachers.

What's your list? You don't have one? Start now. And *breathe*.

ACT 2

THE CONFRONTATION:
Observe

BECOME
THE ALCHEMIST

ON MY JOURNEY, I'VE TRIED SO MANY DIFFERENT METHODS, MODALITIES, and exercises I thought would ease my pain and suffering. I've processed with therapists, men's groups, yogis, empaths, Western and Vedic astrologers, and Tantrikas. Some things worked then didn't, others didn't work at all, and some made me feel worse.

The antidepressants and benzodiazepines that my first psychiatrist prescribed were amazing when I was first introduced to them. They gave me relief, but they were sneaky. I realized I was also using them as an avoidance technique to distract myself from what I was feeling. I put a Band-Aid over a wound that continued to fester.

In the past, whenever something unsettling entered my life, I would sound the alarm bell and run to a doctor or healer. I was so desperate I would give up my power to anyone or anything that promised to relieve my pain. I wanted the quick fix. I then realized it didn't matter how much external input and assistance I received; most of the time, it didn't equate to internal change. It was a short-term solution. I needed to take the input and *do* something with it.

Now, before I reach out for help, I pause and sit with the situation, the emotions, the fear to see if I can work it out on my own. When we know ourselves deeply, we can help ourselves, become our own healers. In order to do that, you need to investigate, observe, and understand your makeup—chemically, emotionally, mentally, physically, and relationally. How can you rearrange, modify, add, or eliminate things in your world to make you the most grounded, calm, peaceful, giving, productive, and loving human being you can be? The distinction here is that you aren't creating an external world to make you safe. Perceived safety (a.k.a. your comfort zone) equals status quo, which equals no growth. You are changing *you* in order to see the world differently.

There's just one problem: humans prefer homeostasis. Driven by our unconscious, we design our lives, more often than not, to maintain safety and certainty. When we get stretched emotionally, physically, and mentally, we crawl back to what is safe. What I am getting at is it's highly likely you are engaging in behaviors that block your progress, keep you stuck, and keep you anxious and fearful under the guise of safety. What you need is to engage in behaviors that push you out of your comfort zone and foster healthy internal change.

Investigate your life. What are you doing to stay safe and certain? And why? Once you know your particular flavor of avoidance, change things up. Challenge yourself. These things often *appear* to be good practices or habits, but even self-care can become over-ritualized and a means of escape from facing life head on and, ultimately, from growing. I've used the gym and meditation as crutches many, many times. When I don't want to intimately *feel* what I'm experiencing in the moment, I may hit the weights or drop onto the mat for twenty minutes of single-pointed focus Shamatha meditation.

Look, these are obviously better outlets than grabbing a shot of whiskey, smoking weed, watching porn, or other more self-destructive methods. But they can still be used to avoid pain and suffering that need to be metabolized through the body. You must tune in and ask yourself, "Am I trying *not* to feel something right now?"

The goal here is to understand your operating system, to hack it, and then to train your physical, emotional, and mental body to be able to withstand more and more stressors and uncertainty. To shed the skin of anxiety and allow for peace and harmony. Maybe, at some point, you'll want to seek out those things that make you uncomfortable and uncertain to desensitize yourself. If you are going to transform yourself, you need to face your most challenging fears. You must bring out your big guns. Everything in this book targets this concept. And it may go against everything you've been taught or heard before.

Alchemy is defined as "the process of taking something ordinary and turning it into something extraordinary, sometimes in a way that cannot be explained."[27] Now, that is something to strive for. Once you understand the building blocks of *you*, you can rearrange them, throw a few out, combine a couple, and restructure yourself into a being who interacts with life from a perspective of safety, security, and love.

Everyone is different. Everyone is affected uniquely by life's circumstances. Everyone has distinct upbringings and events in their lives that have shaped them into who they are today.

The chaos of my childhood household—my mother's mental illness and addiction, my sister's eating disorder, my father's distant and unemotional type-A personality, the responsibility I felt for holding down the fort while my father was frequently away on business, and the lack of emotional support and safety I felt—laid down certain neural pathways in my brain that cause me to process stress and fear, as an adult, in a very different way than other people do. It took me many years before my dam broke. The string of events above created my low self-esteem, my uncertainty about who I was and where I was going in life, my general fear of the world, and my lack of trust in just about everything, which led to my first panic attack that summer day at that beach.

How were *you* shaped? What is working for you, and what isn't? Why are you still doing things that exacerbate your anxieties and avoiding things that bring you calm and peace?

It's often not what is going on in our minds and bodies that is bad. It is our interpretation of those beliefs, thoughts, emotions, and physical feelings. It may be as simple as asking the question, "What am I trying to avoid feeling right now?" Observe your thoughts, your beliefs, and your life.

Sometimes, the stress or anxiety is so intense that sitting with it may be too much, and a good workout will off-gas a chunk of that intensity, calm your mind just a bit, and bring you back to a point where you can actually investigate a little better.

Sometimes, you will need to push yourself to sit with all of it. Each occurrence may require something different. The key is to figure out what makes *you* tick. What are your specific triggers? Get insanely curious about *you*.

If you don't have a starting point and a map, how do you know where you are headed and the best path to get where you want to go? Maybe you need a jumpstart. I am a big proponent of psychotherapy, as long as it's not overdone or used to keep you stuck.

My first psychotherapist changed my life. She became the parent I never had, helping me gently unearth the wounds of my past that created beliefs that were destroying my present life experience in a nurturing and safe environment. In doing so, she equipped me with more tools and awareness. This was a necessary step in my evolution and to get me to a place where I could self-assess and then move into the more challenging modality of trauma therapy.

However, some people get addicted to therapy, and instead of taking responsibility for their lives and moving forward, they keep leaning on others, rehashing their past, and staying victimized. They don't take action. I was one of those people. Eventually, I felt my relationship with my therapist and the progress I was making stagnated. I felt we were treading on a well-worn path, revisiting the same old stories, and no new insights were forthcoming. I still felt like I was *managing* my anxiety. Logically, from the neck up, I knew all the familial mechanics that assisted in my anxiety. But deep within, the roots of that anxiety were still deeply entrenched.

Therapy helped me get to a place of more consciousness quickly. It got me to a point where I was able to make a confident choice to move on and discover other modalities that would assist in taking me deeper. It can be a wonderful way to get some fundamental insights about why you do what you do. It gave me a baseline. I had a chaotic and traumatizing childhood; was taught not to express emotions; and felt broken, less-than, and very unsafe. Experiencing anxiety, for me, made sense.

But therapy isn't the only path to deeper self-understanding. Journaling is a wonderful practice to reveal your inner workings. I have a document I started many years ago titled, simply, "Autobiography." Now and then, I go back in and add things I remember from my past, arranging them from birth to present day. It's quite amazing to go back through it and see how I was shaped over the years.

As a screenwriter, I frequently create character biographies. Most often, 95 percent of this info will never make it into the actual screenplay. Still, the character will emanate a three-dimensional personality because their history pours out of me and onto the page, displayed through their dialogue, actions, and choices. You can use this same process to transform yourself. Write your biography. Dissect your history. Recognize your flaws and gifts (which you may perceive as detriments and what may be holding you back), and use them as fuel to bring to light the *you* that was always there but never allowed to fully blossom. Then, you will have the life you so want for yourself.

Now the shitty part, which I've previously touched upon. So, we feel anxious or panicky, and we want it to end, right? We don't reach for our go-to pain relievers, and our anxiety worsens. We then turn toward the pain, we lean in, which takes us even further out of our comfort zone, which in turn creates more anxiety. You see the problem here: if you turn left and bury the anxiety, it will fester. If you turn right and face it head on, you will create uncertainty and maybe even more anxiety. Either way, the high levels of anxiety are still there. Each path, each choice, *appears* to be really shitty. What do you do?

Well, one thing is certain: if you turn your back on your anxiety, maintain homeostasis, drift through life on autopilot, lean on others excessively, or seek out the quickest pain relief to your anxiety, that is as far as you will go. Sure, you'll put out those neural fires and feel good in the short run, but you are actually strengthening your anxious patterns. It will *never* lessen this way. To be honest, there are times when I look back on my life with envy of the ignorance I had about everything. Although there was uncertainty and pain when I was younger, it felt more diffuse, not so specific, and therefore more manageable. The more I dug into my psychology, the more pain I felt.

There are days now that feel just as bad or worse than the early days of my anxiety. The difference now is knowing what's going on. I know the inner workings of *my* system and why it is reacting the way it is. I do my best not to label what is going on as "wrong" or "right." I have tools. I look at it all from a more aware place. Facing this challenge like a warrior will create more distress but only in the short term. From this place, true alchemy is possible.

A rebirth is afoot. And it's within your power alone to facilitate it.

WHAT IS YOUR ANXIETY EQUATION?

EVERY TIME I WRITE A SCREENPLAY, IT GOES THROUGH MANY, MANY DRAFTS. Usually, the first draft is pretty horrible. But I refine each draft, making it better on every level—from plot to characters to dialogue. Eventually, the script hits on all cylinders and transmits the story I want to tell in a very specific way, eliciting a very specific reaction. Life is good.

As people who suffer from anxiety, we may not realize it, but we have a script that brings us to fear and distress. What we also may not realize is we have the power to revise that script, change our story, and make it an award-winning blockbuster. We anxiety sufferers may all end up in the same place of fear, dread, and panic, but we don't all begin at the same starting point. We are individuals with unique and specific backgrounds.

At first, it seems like anxiety comes out of nowhere, a surge of dark energy that grabs hold of us and won't let go. Our physical, mental, and emotional bodies are deluged with adrenaline and cortisol, and the only thing on our mind is *escape*. Most of this process is not conscious to us. Once you realize this, the most important thing you can do is bring your focus to it and make it conscious.

This surge of anxiety rarely comes out of nowhere. There is usually a step-by-step process that your system goes through to reach this excruciating peak moment. You have a very old script you follow each and every time you reach a state of unease and anxiety. If you can identify it, write it out, it will help you in the process of revising that script. Ask yourself, "What was I thinking right before anxiety took over me?" or, even better, "What event happened that I then perceived a certain way, that I then thought about a certain way, that led to the increase in anxiety?"

The following is an example of an old health-anxiety script I used to run frequently. It's a bit disjointed and might not make complete sense, but I want you to see what I came up with in the moment, when I got curious and asked myself certain questions.

The setup for this story is that right before I felt this specific flavor of anxiety, I was almost always in the same negative mindset: generally feeling down on myself and striving for perfection in *all* areas of my life. I then felt something off in my body, usually something very subtle. This feeling and my skewed mindset set off a swarm of thoughts that would fester in my mind and create further triggers and physical symptoms. The triggers could be about any number of small, ordinary things.

Trigger: My eyesight feels off, blurry.

Response: I used to have a wider angle of vision. How can I be perfect if my vision isn't twenty/twenty? I'm aging, right? I'm terrified of life passing me by. Getting sick, going blind, death.

Trigger: I hear about someone's illness on TV or the radio or read about it on the internet.

Response: Oh no, I've had similar symptoms to this person. Will I get that illness too? I feel less-than, comparing my physical and mental health to others'. My self-esteem plummets.

Trigger: I feel some sort of physical pang in my body or notice some odd way of thinking burrowing into my head.

Response: I hyper-focus on it. Something is wrong. I micromanage my body. I'm hyper-vigilant, focusing on one possible physical or mental issue after another. Like:

- Cancer

- Multiple sclerosis

- Loss of vision

- Loss of hearing

- Heart issues

- Dementia/Alzheimer's

- Shortness of breath

- Stroke

- A dangerous flu

Like the best dramatic scenes on film, the tension builds and the stakes raise. As this happens, the shitstorm in my head blazes into every area of my mind. I'm looking only for the negative. My imagination starts to run wild, uncontrollable. I feel *fear*. Unexplainable fear. And my physical body reacts in kind, creating a disastrous feedback loop. And then the shame slowly builds as a result of going down this stupid path in the first place. My mind starts to wreak havoc. Something is wrong with me physically or mentally. *Should I go to the doctor? Should I get tested for all of the above?* I feel powerless and out of control. Like I have no authority over my mind *or* body. *I can prevent this illness, but only if I do something* now. *If I don't do something* now *and I am* really *sick, I will never forgive myself. And I will die.*

Then, the pendulum swings to beating myself up. *I'm a loser. I'm not a real man. A real man would not have these worries and fears.* And if that just isn't enough, I ramp up the stakes with a set of insane questions that should never be asked at this juncture:

- If I die, how will my family take care of themselves?

- Does my wife think I'm weak?

- Will this fear be with me for the rest of my life?

- Am I going to die before I realize my dreams?

- Am I going to die, and no one will know or care?

So, let's dissect the bizarre scene unfolding above.

All the psychic turmoil above might happen in a split second because it's so deep, so old, and so ingrained. Remember, these seeds were planted when I was very young. I've rehearsed this script hundreds of times before. I know it by heart. The momentum of anxiety is massive and can be unstoppable, shooting off in all directions and enlisting other fears, worries, and concerns, unless we put an abrupt stop to it.

Through a lot of hard work and observation, I learned how to put the brakes on this torture scene straight out of a horror flick, not by interrupting all those pervasive thoughts but by actually learning how to let them and the uncomfortable feelings in my body be and not engage with them, which ultimately lessened their pull and power. I stopped, took a few deep breaths, became aware of my thoughts and the meaning I was giving them, and let it all go. I know, easier said than done, but it *can* be done and will ultimately change your life.

All I wanted to do in the many days and years I suffered with anxiety was make these feelings go away and feel better. Now, I understand that, underneath all this anxiety, because of underlying trauma, part of me was looking for bodily perfection, internally and externally. If one thing appeared to be off (hearing, eye floaters, vision, a pain here or there), it opened the door to worry, fear, and anxiety. I was looking for control. At the core of those fears, the grasping for control, were the much deeper underlying fears we all face: the fear of getting old and, in turn, dying.

Even today, after learning to understand my traumas and deep insecurities and rewriting my script hundreds of times, there is a part of me that does not believe the inner workings of my amazing body will come through for me. I'm in great shape, I take really good care of myself, and I get regular check-ups and have tests and labs performed to back up the idea that I'm in good health. What gives? I've succumbed to a very bad habit: I don't trust myself or the world. This lack of trust developed in me from a very young age. I was given no reason to trust, as my primary caregivers never instilled it in me. Or maybe they did, but it just wasn't enough.

When I get out of this initial mind loop, I sometimes jump to the next fearful or irrational thought: *Well, I may not have something going on just yet, but if I keep thinking this way, I will create an illness.* The same idea as the Law of Attraction. I'm screwed either way. Maybe I am searching for something to make me feel bad, especially when I'm feeling good about myself and my life. Maybe I'm self-prophesying, creating nasty answers to the wrong question: "When is the other shoe going to drop?" Why? Why do I torture myself like this?

This insane process allows me *not* to step into the fullness of my being. It keeps me confused, small, weak, and "safe."

Why and how do *you* torture yourself? What is the process that brings you to anxiety and panic? You need to find out.

In your most challenging moments and times, try to:

1. Observe and notice the mental patterns and internal dialogue.

2. Ask yourself what emotions are coming up because of these mental patterns.

3. Label the emotions: FEARFUL, ANXIOUS, SAD, or FRUSTRATED.

4. Then, feel them in your body.

5. Sit with the feelings, breathe, slow down, and go within.

6. Ride the wave of discomfort, and…let go. Let go. Let go.

I do my best to slow down instead of feeding my desire to speed up.

We need to fill in the grooves we created in our minds long ago, during childhood and adolescence.

Like a screenwriter, playwright, or storyteller, you need to "beat out" short, descriptive bullet points that outline the steps you go through to bring yourself to a high level of anxiety. When this script is in front of you and not swirling around in your head, you can very clearly see how the journey of your anxiety plays out from beginning to end. Then you can rewrite your life script. Make it better, replacing anxiety, dread, and fear with new responses that take you to a more joyful, peaceful, and confident place.

DUDE, WHERE'S MY BODY?

MY ANXIETY EQUATION BECAME CLEARER TO ME A FEW YEARS BACK, DURING a period of time that seemed like an eternity, when I experienced something I would say fell on the extreme end of anxiety symptoms. I had actually experienced it when I was younger, but in early 2016, it came back much more intensely. I felt completely disconnected from my body for extended periods of time.

It's called "depersonalization" and is often experienced by those taking recreational drugs. The fact that I am stone-sober during these episodes makes them even more terrifying. Sometimes, my sensations are coupled with derealization, where everything around me feels foggy, unreal, and dreamlike. It's quite hard to describe the experience with words alone.

The Mayo Clinic describes these symptoms as follows: "Depersonalization-derealization disorder occurs when you persistently or repeatedly have the feeling that you're observing yourself from outside your body or you have a sense that things around you aren't real, or both."[28]

At the time, I was dealing with some major outside stressors. My mother was displaying some erratic behavior that resembled early-stage dementia, I was about to file a very large and complicated international lawsuit, and I was questioning the direction of my life. I was very nihilistic at the time and thought I may be having some sort of breakdown. Susanne M., the spiritual mentor I reached out to, gave me some perspective. She confirmed this was more than a simple anxiety-disorder-related symptom and sounded like something more in line with a spiritual crisis.

Things have now settled down, but even today, I periodically struggle with this bizarre symptom. I feel like I'm floating just outside my body, only connected by a slim tether. Alternatively, I can feel completely removed, detached, like I am literally slipping out of my skin and into an abyss, away from reality and myself. There's nothing for me to grab onto. I touch myself to make sure I'm still actually here, on this planet.

For those of you who can relate to this, I want to provide you some relief. I have come to realize it's just a symptom, a really bad one. This took me a while to dissect and understand. It cannot and will not hurt you, ever, unless you let it. I now continually remind myself of this reality.

I believe this symptom is directly tied to the anxiety sufferer's need to control. I mean, what could be worse than completely losing the most fundamental of controls: your body, mind, and reality?

What I have come to understand is that part of what is going on here is my mind has reached a stress/anxiety tipping point and started to alter or cut off certain normal bodily functions. These could be cognitive, brain, or physical functions. This is explained succinctly in an article published by the National Association on Mental Illness on depersonalization:[29]

> Extreme stress may not lead to "fight" or "flight." Instead, this heightened arousal can lead to dissociation, or a disruption in brain functioning, in order to emotionally distance yourself from a perceived life-threatening situation. Your mind shuts down to protect itself from being overwhelmed. However, being in this state makes us feel disconnected from our environment and the people around us.

Trauma was the culprit. When I was a child, I dissociated from myself because it was too damn painful to feel the feelings I was feeling in the moment. So now, when stress or overwhelm come into play, my body takes a vacation, just like it did when I was very young.

I go into what feels like fight-or-flight mode as my body and mind try to protect me. My body pulls in all resources, including vital brain functions, and in the process, creates this foreign, bizarre experience akin to an LSD trip.

This is similar to when the body experiences freezing-cold temperatures. All the blood is pulled to the vital organs, the parts of you that keep you alive, which may cause complete loss of feeling in the extremities.

As my depersonalization symptoms persisted, I really began to question my sanity. It was such a fearful experience, one that I expected regularly. This bad habit became a self-fulfilling prophecy.

Understanding what was going on, the script I was playing out, required me to pay very close attention and discern what was make-believe and what was real. I wasn't going mad. I was once told that people who are going mad or having a psychotic episode don't know they have temporarily lost the plot and most likely won't remember when they come back to reality.

Now, I just remind myself this is what is going on, make a point to ground and feel my body, and ride the wave of unreality.

When confronted with this wild symptom, close your eyes, place your feet firmly on the ground, and breathe deeply.

The sensations you are experiencing may be so intense that sitting or standing still is just not possible. That's ok. Just knowing this craziness is another symptom and pinning a flag to that notion may be enough.

Water is a miracle worker. It's very soothing, cleansing, and grounding. Take a bath, and discover for yourself.

Reassure yourself this is just a passing storm.

I know this sounds so basic and simple, but it's really what you need to do.

When my spiritual mentor and I talked about my depersonalization, she told me that when experiencing depersonalization, I should recognize I've become diffuse and my identity, or at least what I believe is my identity, an anxious identity born at a very young age, may be falling away, and I should rest in that. Although it feels strange and frightening, I am actually becoming more of who I really am.

Labeling it is very effective. It takes the power out of what could be a debilitating symptom.

Dissociation may be required to allow the disintegration of the old you and coalescence of the new you.

Ground yourself, be present, observe, be patient, and trust. It really comes down to how we perceive what is going on.

THE KIDS ARE...NOT ALRIGHT

When I was young, I wanted to be a rock star, and before that, a pilot. I learned to play the guitar at a young age, jamming with friends for hours. The iconic band I was most drawn to was the Who. It was their freedom, their abandon, their power and raw energy that fascinated me, including their tendency to destroy all their equipment during shows (back when doing so wasn't as fashionable as it is nowadays). I was particularly inspired by the lead guitarist, Pete Townshend. He was the one usually leading the charge of destruction.

According to Townshend, his song *The Kids Are Alright* is about taking chances in life, trying to work out right and wrong through all the things he did as he moved from childhood to adulthood. It's a testament to the fact that despite all the crazy things he did on stage, in his marriage, and to his body, which, on reflection, might seem quite irresponsible, he ultimately turned out ok. I believe he may have been onto something.

I'm not saying we should all emulate Mr. Townshend, but the nugget of gold here is that freeing abandon, leaping into the unknown, and taking chances, both emotional and physical, are good for our souls. A life without abandon leads to stagnation, boredom, stress, and anxiety. And it's not just rock stars who think this way. William H. Danforth, who founded the Nestlé Purina company, published a book more than ninety years ago titled *I Dare You!* in which he urged readers of any age to take chances and fulfill their full potential through his strategies and becoming more risk seeking.

I now believe I chose the life of an artist because it safely gives me that sense of abandon and freedom. But most of us today don't live like the Who or Mr. Danforth; we are mired in anxiety. A 2017 *New York Times* article, "Prozac Nation Is Now the United States of Xanax," says the current youth, specifically between the ages of thirteen and seventeen, are more anxious and depressed than at any other time in our country's history.[30] Why is this?

Certainly, the recent pandemic has only exacerbated this problem. A 2021 article in the *Lancet*, a weekly peer-reviewed science journal, states, "Before 2020, mental disorders were leading causes of the global health-related burden, with depressive and anxiety disorders being leading contributors to this burden. The emergence of the COVID-19 pandemic has created an environment where many determinants of poor mental health are exacerbated."[31]

There are myriad causes you could blame for this rise in anxiety. The societal focus on extrinsic goals, the uncertain domestic political climate, too much input from the world around us, and the overwhelming speed at which information is delivered, including the rise of social media, are among the causes cited. In regards to the pandemic, I would add a lack of perceived control, lack of perceived safety, and lack of trust. But the interesting part of the *Times* article is the finding that the lack of play, self-exploration, and adventure—the abandon that Pete Townshend talked about—is a big contributor to the declining mental states of children.

So this ever-increasing mental-health problem has more to do with the subjective view these children have of themselves in the world and less to do with what is going on in the world. Boom. There it is. *Perception.*

How each child or adult observes the world and themselves in it is the key to understanding why they are so much more anxious than in the past. The good news? *We* have the ability to shift our reality. Most of the time, because of our evolutionary path, our worldview leans toward the negative, which is very dark and scary. So a good place to start would be to observe and get clear on what is *actually* happening in our world. Remember the "The Work" by Byron Katie:[32]

1. Is my thought/reality true? (Yes or no. If no, move to 3.)

2. Can I absolutely know it's true? (Yes or no.)

3. How do I react, what happens, when I *believe* that thought/reality?

4. Who would I be *without* that thought/reality?

Most of the time, the answer to Number 2 is "no." Further grounding ourselves and getting present is the first step in tuning in to our reality and our place in it.

On that note, let's revisit Pete Townshend's story. I recently found out he has admitted the reason for his theatrics was he genuinely felt he wasn't that great of a guitarist, so he had to make up for it with performance art. Can that be true? One of the most revered and celebrated guitarists on the planet thought he just wasn't that great, that his skills were lacking, so he compensated with theatrics, but we, the audience, thought we were watching the birth of one of the greatest guitarists of all time. *And* we *were right.*

It's all about perception. Never forget that your own perceptions of the world are not necessarily how it is. Nor are they how the world sees you. Anyone suffering from anxiety right now has the power to reframe their fearful and anxious self-perceptions by allowing more room for play, mistakes, self-love, and risk without becoming an attention-grabbing asshole.

ANXIETY MAKES ME FEEL IMPORTANT

ANXIETY GIVES ME SIGNIFICANCE. AND IF I'M NOT CAREFUL, IT CAN BECOME my identity again.

My mother and sister would frequently fight about who had the more significant emotional problems because whoever had more shit going on would get the most attention. None of this was conscious, but it certainly was noticeable to me. We all do this on some level, for attention, for sympathy, for compassion, or to straight up manipulate. Even though it may sound backward-ass, a "disorder" piques interest, and people want to help. They pay attention. It's concrete, it's real, it's frightening, and it's interesting.

People are attracted to scary stuff, just like we're drawn to bad news. Why do you think people are so intrigued by horror movies? This is why people often choose victimhood over taking action. It is why I initially chose victimhood. If we are sick or hurting, it draws people in. The attention we get from telling people all about our anxiety may be the most attention we ever get. And it feels good. It's soothing. A panic attack is like the light that attracts the moth.

We need to notice and then stop the manipulation. And remember, we are all important. We don't need the anxiety label to support that notion. Nobody is perfect, but you should strive to have your positivity, your kindness, your vulnerability, and your humanness be what attracts people, not your negativity.

PERFECT IS THE ENEMY OF GOOD...AND PEACE OF MIND

I'VE TRIED DESPERATELY TO CONTROL MY LIFE, WHICH INCLUDED SHOOT-ING for some bizarre version of perfection. My efforts for control have ranged from strict routines to endless to-do lists to a very obsessive no-fat/no-salt diet to attempting to control my significant other (mostly in manipulative ways like passive-aggressive behavior). My thinking at the time was if I did these specific things, manipulating externals, I would magically be able to bend reality to my will, which in turn would allow me to control my insides, my emotions, my feelings, and, ultimately, my world. All would be "perfect."

Here is the inner dialogue that usually runs through the minds of perfectionists: "If I am perfect, I won't be challenged. How can you challenge perfection? If I am perfect, I will be deeply loved. If I am perfect, I will breeze through life. If I am perfect, I will be looked up to, idolized, wildly successful, and anxiety and stress free." Well, breaking news: that never goes as planned. There is no such thing as perfection. Your lofty goals end up being futile and feed the anxiety engine.

If I strive for perfection to ward off uncomfortable feelings and I miss the mark (which I always will because perfection doesn't exist), anxiety creeps in, and then I become even more hyper-vigilant. The pattern loops and gets ingrained.

Writer, historian, and philosopher Voltaire was onto something when he said, "Perfect is the enemy of good."[33] If we are only satisfied with unattainable perfection, we will procrastinate and judge as the good and even great pass us by like a leaf on a river.

Perfectionism, anxiety, and fear tend to go hand in hand. Obsessive Compulsive Disorder (challenge) is often also in the mix and frequently tends to show up in anxiety sufferers. I struggle with all four.

Perfectionitis can show up in obvious ways, like, in my case, having my day planned out to the second. I used to do this to fill my day in an effort to ward off any potential anxiety.

Now there is nothing wrong with scheduling out your day. To be honest, my present daily routine looks very similar to the one I used to have when I over scheduled. The difference is that now I don't fall into fear, which in the past would blossom into anxiety and then lead to panic, when one thing in my day needs to be shifted, someone runs late, or something unexpectedly pops up that needs my attention. Back when I clung to my schedule so vigorously, my perfect day could quickly unravel and become not so perfect.

This behavior can show up in more subtle ways, such as using what appears to be others' perfection to measure my own life and realizing I'm not perfect. Surprise, I'm not!

Sometimes, I'll scroll through an entertainment-industry website and see mostly the highlights from writers, directors, peers, and all the people I look up to, and I begin to measure my very real, imperfect life against theirs, which appear to be full of ease and perfection. I distance myself from them. I put them way up high on the mountaintop and dig a grave for myself. At the same time, I strive for that same perceived perfection.

This leads to envy, frustration, self-loathing, and more anxiety.

I incorrectly believe the people I read about and look up to are perfect, get all the breaks, are so much smarter than me, and are more talented than me. To quell this anxiety, I search and search, obsessively, to find anything negative about that individual because if I can find that chink in the armor, which I always will (because you can find anything on the internet! And remember, no one is perfect), for some strange reason, it makes me feel better. It's like I am proving to myself they are not perfect, which is obvious logically, but when I am on an obsessive, perfectionist, anxiety-fueled roll, it's not that obvious.

And the interesting thing is just like we can project our flaws onto others because we don't want to acknowledge them in ourselves, we can also project our gold, our power, our amazing abilities onto others as well. So those things you are so envious of in others may already exist in yourself—you just can't see it.

Comparison as a way to fuel your perfectionism is a lost cause. It's a waste of time, a lot of time, and only ends up exacerbating the frustration, envy, and even self-hatred we desperately want to distance ourselves from. French author and moralist François de la Rochefoucauld said it beautifully: "Our envy always lasts longer than the happiness of those we envy."[34]

Observe your behaviors in this area. Where are you incredibly hard on yourself, striving for perfection, to keep yourself safe and therefore stuck? Know that you are imperfectly perfect. It's what makes you interesting. Tweaking your insides—your emotions, your reactions, your self-talk— *will* allow you to change your reality, your outside world. Strive to be the best you can, for excellence. And realize your imperfections, your flaws, make you unique. They can be teachers and guides and foster you into becoming the best version of yourself: a self free of anxiety.

CONFIRMATION B.S.

I WANT MY FEARS TO BE REAL. EACH AND EVERY SOUL-SUCKING, MIND-BOG-gling, terrifying, shameful fear. Because if I truly believe they are not real, and let's face it, they are not, I will have to accept the fact I've been living a lie. And if I've been living a lie, I'll need to question why I haven't realized it's a lie.

Man, I must be stupid not to be able to figure out that certain fears I have are complete bullshit. That's it. I'm just not intelligent enough to catch this incorrect interpretation of life. I have wasted all these years for nothing. I'm a piece of shit. You see the wormhole that sends you down? I personally don't want to feel all that pain, shame, and less-than-itis. But I am abso-lutely willing to sit with the pain of unsubstantiated fear.

I continue to search out all the evidence that proves my fears are real and cut off everything (including all data) that proves they are not. Because that false evidence keeps me safe, safe in the knowledge that my thoughts, beliefs, and understandings are correct. They are scary, but they are right. So my mind must be working correctly, and I can trust it. This gives me certainty. As I've said before, change is scary, even if that change will actually pull you out of your personal hell and ultimately produce *less* fear.

My antenna is up and ready to receive anything and everything that aligns with my negative, fearful beliefs and thoughts about who I am and what I struggle with. It could be a simple look from an innocent bystander, maybe words, a whisper, the energy in a room. If you are really good, you can turn positive intel into negative. I could! A kind compliment about you gets flipped into, *They're just saying that to make me feel good. They don't really mean that. They feel sorry for me.* Or worse, *This person is trying to get an angle on me. I don't trust them.* We will look for anything to stoke and keep alive the fears that have become our second skin.

You'll see this play out in people's reactions to films, books, and other media. If an individual loves a particular filmmaker, they may look past all the flaws of a film and convince themselves of what a great piece of art that film is, even if it's actually a piece of crap. Conversely, an individual may really dislike a filmmaker/film and find a litany of flaws in what may be a masterpiece. This bias is something I still struggle with, but it's definitely not as intrusive as it has been in the past. Deep presence and questioning thoughts, beliefs, behaviors, and pretty much everything in your perceived reality are helpful. Not in an obsessive way; in a smart way.

You have to understand you want to see and hear the internal movie you want to see, the one you've been watching for many years. Maybe not "you," the part of you that is sacred, untouched, and eternal, but that scared, little you that needs to perpetuate the lie in order to feel safe—safe in misery. And you'll find others to confirm your movie as well. This is not observing. Observation requires some distance and objectivity. Most of your fears are *not* real; they're a bunch of B.S. Start confirming this now.

ANXIETY
LOVES COMPANY

IN MY LATE TEENS, WHEN I FIRST STARTED TO STRUGGLE WITH ANXIETY, I *thought* I simply wanted to turn my brain off and for everyone and everything around me to be chill. I *thought* I just wanted some peace and calm and to not feel like my brain was on fire all the time. Consciously, that is certainly what I wanted. But unconsciously, there was a very different need at play. Looking back, the truth is, in a strange way, I felt more comfortable when I was on edge. When everyone and everything around me was anxiety provoking, I felt at home.

You see, if everyone else stays on the same level—anxious—or sticks to the status quo—not showing anyone else that change and freedom *are* possible—then we can all stay stuck, freaked out, and in our imaginary safety bubble together. Even though consciously, I would fight against this idea, I was battling my stronger unconscious that wanted anxiety and chaos to reign. And it succeeded by causing me to believe I was safe and would be less anxious staying at the same level.

Over time, as I've gone through the expected rituals of life—going to college, entering the real world, marriage, intimacy—I've noticed this in many areas of my life. However, staying at this homeostasis level keeps the anxiety alive. We actually make an attempt to recruit people down to our level because we believe that will make everything better.

In the chapter "PERFECT IS THE ENEMY OF GOOD…AND PEACE OF MIND," I spoke about idealizing others' success and how I use perceived perfection to beat myself up. This is not that. Here, when comparison and envy, which are big anxiety instigators for me, creep into my headspace, I want to bring those targets of my envy *down to my level.* I know, it's absolutely nuts. One moment, I am crucifying myself for not having the success that others enjoy, and the next moment, I am trying to minimize their achievements, their lives, in order to feel ok. Usually, these individuals are living the life I *think* I want. To be more specific, they are individuals who are doing exactly what I want to do: living a filmmaker's life, collaborating with creatives on amazing projects, winning accolades, and making a lot of money in the process. I feel horrible about saying this, but I want them to suffer too. I want them to be sad about their place in life. I want to know they are just as insecure as I am. It gives me a sense of self-satisfaction.

There is a term for this. It's called "schadenfreude," and it is the pleasure I derive from another's struggle, failure, or misfortune instead of saying, "Wow, that's impressive, how can I lift myself up to what I perceive as success?" or "How can I achieve what they have achieved? What could I learn from this person? How could I model myself after them? What are they doing that I'm not?"

That second path requires way more work and, most likely, anxiety. It requires me to take an honest look at myself and break out of the old patterns and habits that keep me stuck. It requires change, maybe big change, and that creates massive anxiety. The anxiety generated through comparison and envy is my realization there is a perceived gap between where I am and where I want to be. I must grow there. And that is scary.

What's really interesting is that what I am recognizing in another person, the positive attribute that I long for, most likely is a part of me that has remained stuck in myself, hidden. It's not fully realized. And I cannot see that part in me. But I can see it in others. Again, I need to change that part of me, allow it to blossom, to become the person I ultimately want to be. Ironically, it's a futile psychological process. Many of the individuals I fawn over suffer, feel sadness, envy, and feel deep insecurity—even at their levels of success.

Change threatens the safety of your anxiety cocoon. So, there's the rub. It also creates anxiety but only temporarily.

Remember, as crazy as it may sound, we like our anxiety.

You know you do. And this realization probably pisses you off. I know it pissed me off when I finally had it.

Just like misery, if everyone else around us is anxious, it's easier to accept it in ourselves. Maybe it makes you feel a little less self-critical, like you're a little less stuck if you're surrounded by other people who are stuck too, maybe more stuck than you. Not to mention how you can all sit around the campfires of purgatory, chatting about your anxiety, how bad it is, how it will never end, and on and on and on, perpetuating the anxiety, which concretizes it and makes us feel at home.

Nuts, I know.

Remember, we cast the film of our life. Everything from relationships to situations have been perfectly set up (by us!) to keep our anxiety alive.

So, on one hand, we breathe deeply, meditate, and eat right, and on the other hand, we drink pots of coffee and too much alcohol, watch (bad) news, don't get enough sleep, and surround ourselves with depressing, neurotic individuals.

That is kinda insane, right?

Understand, this is usually happening unconsciously, under the radar. The reason we do it is there is a part of us that wants to keep that security blanket of anxiety alive. Who would we be without it? And when the only other option *also* produces anxiety, what are we to do? Well, one thing is certain: the security-blanket option will continually produce the result we've already achieved, more anxiety. The other option may produce short-term anxiety, but it will ultimately break us free from it.

You can be the one to break the mold, to show people what's possible, even if at first, it may make others *more* anxious because their stagnant state is being threatened by the calm, clear, focused, loving state they so dearly long for. Those people who kept you comfortable will soon despise and envy *you*. Because they don't want you to change either, as it threatens their safe, stuck lives.

You have two choices: remain stuck with all the other victims and sufferers in an endless anxiety loop, *or* go out on a limb and change, take personal responsibility, and face your uncertainties, which will also create anxiety for you and others but only for a short time. Anxiety either way, yes. But one is temporary and a doorway to freedom. I decided to be free and show myself what was possible. You should too.

DON'T B-LAME

I HAD A ROUGH CHILDHOOD, EMOTIONALLY AND MENTALLY. I WISH IT could have been different. But what I will not do is look back and blame my present state of affairs—my stresses and my anxieties—on my parents or my upbringing. I will not play the victim. Of course, arriving at this understanding took a lot of time, patience, deep observation, introspection, and self-love.

I am not a child anymore. I have diligently worked through my deep wounds and traumas, and now, I have a wealth of knowledge and tools that allow me to see my present reality clearly. I believe the constitution, compassion, fight-for-the-underdog spirit, and determination I now have are the direct results of the obstacles I was up against as a child and adolescent.

This is not to excuse my parents' lack of parenting skills or emotional support. Not at all. They fucked up, plain and simple. I actually verbalized my unhappiness to my mother recently, and she responded to me with, "I don't know what else to say except, I'm sorry." It was only ten words. That's all I got. But I felt it. I knew my mom, at that moment, meant it. And I wasn't going to push her any further because I knew I wasn't going to get much more. She would most likely deflect with a mention of the weather or the untimely death of a friend or relative. The entire conversation was over in less than ten minutes.

Here's the thing. My mother and father didn't point at my crib and go, "Let's fuck this kid's life up." They didn't hope I would develop debilitating anxiety and have to struggle through life. They had a lot of crap on their plates. And they probably did the best they could to raise their two children. They did what they could with what they had. I'm sure they raised us the way they did in part because of the way *they* were raised—and my grandparents did what *they* did because of the way *they* were raised.

Not too long ago, I still held a lot of anger and resentment toward my parents. It has lessened. It's still there, but it doesn't grip me so hard. One of my desires when speaking to my mother about how I felt about my childhood was to let her know that, although the past is now written in stone, we can easily modify the future. We can connect more deeply and grow emotionally closer. But I can't do it on my own.

One thing I didn't want was for my mother to leave her physical body without knowing exactly how I felt about my childhood and our relationship. Unfortunately, that was the case with my father. He died way too young, and I never was able to dive deep with him. I felt there was no closure, which created a void where blame could fester. Blame keeps you frozen in the past, causing you *not* to take responsibility for the present.

You know what happens when you don't take responsibility? You don't feel like you have any control over your situation, your life. And that creates anxiety. This concept works both ways. When we are feeling anxious, we blame.

Blame is a negative thinking pattern that's been engrained into your DNA and results in sadness and fear. Don't be a victim; don't blame. This doesn't mean to live in denial of your present or past. Understand what happened, be angry, be kind to yourself, make peace with past traumas, and vocalize your truth to the individuals who hurt you and maybe shaped you. And then move on. Stop living out a story that isn't happening anymore. Take responsibility for the present.

YOU'VE BEEN TRAINED TO BE ANXIOUS

I TRAINED MYSELF TO BE SCARED AND FEARFUL AND TO LACK CONFIDENCE. I did a really good job of it. That is one thing I am truly confident about.

What were my worst negative thought processes?

Blurred vision = brain tumor

Tightness in chest = imminent heart attacks

Foggy or forgetful mind = dementia

Feeling outside of my body = schizophrenia or impending nervous breakdown

Father dies from cancer = I will die from cancer

Every time my fear arose, I backed away. Every time my critical mind berated me, I believed it. Every time I failed at something, I chalked it up to something inherently wrong with me. Every time deep emotions welled up in me, which always triggered fear, I stuffed them down because I'm a man, and men, according to my father's representation of masculinity, don't express sadness, fear, or insecurity.

I've compared myself to others, beat myself up when I didn't measure up, and even when I had little wins and successes, I usually didn't celebrate them. Most of the time, I told myself I could have done more, better, faster. Each and every time I gave in, believing this nonsense, I was deepening the grooves and strengthening toxic habits. It became an identity for me, a warm, comfortable blanket of everything I tricked myself into believing.

The more I avoided situations that instilled anxiety (e.g., an important phone call, intimacy, a plane ride, an event, a presentation, an interaction with someone else), the stronger the fear reflex (run and avoid) got. This process can lead to phobias. If it gets really bad, you can just think of the situation or interaction, and it will spark an anxious reaction.

A few years ago, when I was on what I thought was the razor's edge of sanity, my mind and body were coming apart at the seams, and I didn't think either of them would survive. I had experienced anxiety my whole life, but this felt like next-level shit. I felt agoraphobic, depersonalized, and at a high level of anxiety on a regular basis.

I reverted to old patterns and thought I just may need some medication. I reached out to my wife, my therapist, and others I trusted deeply, and they told me, "Ok, maybe you do, but why not go against the grain? Sit with the torture for a bit, maybe a week, see what happens, what it tells you. Be with it. Lean into it."

That is what I did, as best I could. I made an agreement with myself that I would pause and then explore this pain and terror more deeply. I went back to my toolbox and prioritized my daily spiritual practice a bit more, which included breathwork, meditation, and physical workouts.

This unbelievably rough time in my life allowed me to discover that every-thing I need to battle this challenge boils down to a handful of simple concepts: breathing, watching, observing, understanding my thoughts, feeling, and letting go. For me, feeling and letting go were big ones. I trusted that my constitution was way stronger than I was giving it credit for and that I was not alone in this terror. I was being supported by some-thing bigger than myself. I just needed to lean into *that* when all else felt lost. I also knew that at any point in time, I could reach out for professional help. I had a team of trusted advisors. The process wasn't perfect by any means. There were days I really questioned my ability to continue on.

So, let's dig in a bit deeper. How do you deal with this old conditioning? How do you untrain yourself of anxiety-inducing behaviors? How can you shift your responses to perceived fear? First, you must desensitize yourself.

DISCLAIMER: This will be scary. And *you can do it*.

There are two methods: baby steps (systematic), *or* jump into the deep end (flooding). They both work.

"Feel the fear...and do it anyway,"[35] author Susan Jeffers says in her land-mark self-help book of the same title. Everything in your body and mind will tell you to walk away, give in, and succumb to the anxiety. But remem-ber, it's a lie. It's old. It's conditioned.

Today, I continue to lean in and have faith. And I'm still here. I didn't go on meds. I didn't snap. Making it through that hell only strengthened my resolve. This was a huge accomplishment and a testament to what I've been preaching in this book. It may get ugly, really ugly, but it will pass.

Your mind can be sneaky. It'll say, "You need to distract yourself! You can't do this! This is the worst it's ever been! Before it was not as bad, so you could deal with it, but this time, you had better call for help!" Lie after lie after lie. And you listen. You believe. And when you do, you reinforce your conditioning.

The best plan of action? Sit with it. My confidants were right. Discover where the fear lives in your body, and let it tell you what it is trying to tell you. Don't try to figure it out. This isn't an intellectual process. That only increases your anxiety. As strange as it sounds, if you breathe, watch, and become curious, things start to settle down. Your goal is to break the relentless, habitual cycle.

I'm not saying this is the plan for *every* situation. Sometimes, you really may need to take care of yourself. Sometimes, you'll need to back away and seek shelter. Sometimes, you should seek professional help. Sometimes, you'll need medication to get you through a very difficult time. I firmly believe these options should only be utilized temporarily, not permanently. No matter what you do, you should be kind to yourself. Tell yourself what a wonderful job you did facing this thing that frightens you so much.

Next time you face it, you'll be able to sit with it a bit longer. The key here is if you do choose to back away, you shouldn't beat yourself up. Instead, rejoice; pat yourself on the back because that dark forest ahead that puts the fear of God in you just got a little less dense and a bit brighter. This is a win, not a loss.

Maybe at first, you sit with the uncomfortable feelings for just a few minutes. Then next time, ten minutes. After that, twenty.

You can slowly metabolize fear and anxiety.

So breathe deeply. Pay really close attention to what is going on inside your body. Feel the pain down to its roots. This takes a big commitment and patience, as you are reprogramming your nervous system. It's a complete unlearning. It will take some time to shift this all in the other direction. That is ok. Because little by little, things will shift, and you will feel better and better.

You need to update your internal system constantly. These are bad habits you've developed over years, maybe decades. They are now deeply ingrained.

In the past, I reacted when I should have responded. About to get on a plane or walk into a movie theater? Fear. About to jump into the blank screenplay page? Dread. About to pick up the phone and confront the last person on earth I want to confront? No!

That is why I recommend a full year of experimentation, which I will outline at the end of this book.

The cool thing is this desensitization will help you in so many areas of your life. All those things that felt so uncomfortable for you to do or face also get metabolized and reframed. New perceptions are birthed and cemented.

In your personal life, your professional life, and your spiritual life, when you pay attention, you realize how much you avoid and react on a daily basis. I now know that what I went through a few years ago has given me clarity about the specific tools I need to face almost anything. It's been a distillation process. All the years, different modalities, and practices have brought me to a simple, powerful trio that is amazingly effective: *Breathe, Observe, and Let Go.*

Facing down your fears will make your life so much bigger. You will create fear-bashing muscles in the process. A cool experiment is to ask yourself when you're feeling fear or anxiety, "What would I be feeling, doing, accomplishing right now if I wasn't feeling this fear? Or if the possibility of failure didn't exist?" The answers that come up may surprise you.

It's time to reprogram your system holistically, not through medications or other things I believe serve only as Band-Aids.

I know there will be people who will say, "But it's unbearable, and I can't do it. I've tried so hard, and nothing has worked." I would ask you to ask yourself if that is *really* the truth because to me, it sounds like the anxiety and fear speaking, not the deepest part of you that is untouchable, imperturbable.

This is not an easy path and will take time and patience; however, it is simple. Simple processes, tactics, and practices. Simplicity, in and of itself, eases the pangs of anxiety. If I did it, a neglected, shy, insecure kid from a dysfunctional family who had big dreams and tons of rejection and heartbreak, who figured he would never amount to anything, if *I* faced my most terrifying inner demons and succeeded in crafting a beautiful life on so many levels, you can do it too. I have no special powers you don't have.

PUT YOUR LIFE
IN REVERSE

About a year ago, I went on a silent retreat in the San Gabriel mountains, and what I realized is just how damn plugged in I was. To news, to the internet, to endless to-do lists and mind chatter. The withdrawal I experienced was intense, frightening. My anxiety surged because the calm, quiet, and inactivity were so hard for my system to deal with. I was with myself and had nothing else.

I have no problem quieting my mind for two twenty-five-minute meditation sessions a day, but eight to ten hours a day was a harrowing experience. I sunk into paranoia, negative self-talk, and tremendous anxiety. Since I couldn't speak, read, or distract myself in any of the normal ways I would when off the mountain, the experience was very confronting. When I told the Buddhist teacher Marv T. of my situation during our mini check-in, he smiled and said, "Great, you're starting to cook!"

Apparently, this was a good thing. As I hesitantly walked into the meditation Zendo, a rectangular, wooden, cabin-like structure, I was prepping for battle. I mustered up all my warrior tools, chose the same spot I always did, fluffed and arranged my cushions and blanket, and dropped onto my ass. As soon as I did and closed my eyes, the thoughts and fears exploded.

Like the cockroaches, bugs, and other creepy-crawlies that come to life in the darkness, all those things I thought would come up for me did. They were waiting for me, for the opportune time to strike. However, this time, I trusted the process, breathed, and let go. Soon after, those mind demons drifted into the background, and then they pretty much disappeared. I then had one of the most blissful experiences I'd ever had in my meditation practice. I had entered the first jhānas. No worries, no anxiety, no fear. Only blissful sensations throughout my body.

What I believe my teacher noticed in me was that this was the darkness before the light. My water was about to boil. It was a good thing, and if I just let it be, stopped trying to figure it all out and complicate things, relief and insight would come.

On the mountain that day, in that very quiet, wooden edifice among a group of other determined practitioners, they did. My teacher was right. The main insight I had was that quieting the mind, pulling away from all worldly distractions, makes the inner world louder, scarier, and generally more unstable. However, if you sit with it, with all of it, and let it burn itself out, it will ultimately become so still and quiet it will transmute into bliss. Right then, I knew if it was possible there, in the Zendo, it was possible anywhere.

We need to go back to basics, to simplicity.

Back in the '70s, there were three channels, no cell phones, and no internet. When we wanted to see a movie, we actually went to the theater, and we had to wait until the next day to get the previous day's news. Life in general moved at a much slower pace. Life was manageable. Our minds were less full.

Maybe if you are a millennial or part of Gen Z, your anxiety just spiked at the thought of disconnecting. *What would I do? How would I live my life? Not connected 24/7? Impossible.* You can handle it. Moreover, you will benefit from the practice immediately.

I would argue the reason many people are so anxious is because they are connected 24/7. And I'm not just talking about the constant busyness and multitasking of modern life. It's also the quality of the content we are ingesting through all these sources. It's mostly negative or fosters negativity. Try and take mini breaks and fasts from the busy world around you.

When you turn off and unplug from everything around you, all the inputs, your insides get really loud. That's the interesting side effect. And ultimately, this is precisely why we distract ourselves. It's like someone slammed on the brakes of our lives. It's really hard just to be with ourselves, our thoughts, and our bodily sensations. We just don't want to hear or look at ourselves too closely. What might we find? But those innermost thoughts and feelings, stuffed down deep, are part of the problem and the seeds that bloom into some of our most stubborn anxieties.

So unplug from everything, and listen carefully to the things that bubble up from the inside. They may have something to teach you. Don't look away in disgust from pain (physical or emotional) or grasp for a joyous or pleasurable thought. Just let them all be. Once the hard lessons are learned, digested, felt, and reframed, they won't trouble you anymore. They will evaporate.

WHAT'S THE WORST
THAT CAN HAPPEN?

Seneca the Younger said, "If an evil has been pondered beforehand, the blow is gentle when it comes."[36]

Premeditatio malorum, or the imagining of things that could go wrong or bring us harm, was a very popular, two-thousand-year-old Stoic practice. It's sort of like controlled and focused negative thinking. The logic is that if we are prepared for setbacks and disasters, it'll soften their effects if and when they come.

You see how I said "if"? Most of our apocalyptic fears do not come to fruition.

My therapist, Dr. M., taught me the following process that builds on this Stoic concept. She asked, "What is your biggest fear? Humiliation? Failure? Abandonment? Or is it more intense? Heart attack? Losing your mind? Death?"

"To be honest, I've struggled with all of these," I told her. "And the combos are the toughest ones. What if I snap and lose my shit before I realize my dreams?"

She said, "What if you do?"

I didn't have an answer for her immediately. Then I realized, if I snapped, literally lost my mind, I might not be aware of anything. If I wasn't aware of anything, how could I feel sadness or pain? How could I feel anything? Shit, maybe it wouldn't be so bad. I then asked myself, *What if I have a heart attack? What would happen? How would it happen?* I know, not a happy thought. But I was there to challenge myself, right?

Of course, having a heart attack would be a horrible experience. It doesn't necessarily mean I would die. But what about the excruciating pain I might feel? And what if I did die? Then what? I wouldn't be able to experience *life* anymore. I wouldn't be able to take care of my family; my loved ones; my wife; my cat, Joey; and my dog, Stella. Would I ever see any of them again? I then went back to my earlier question. *If I was dead, would I be aware of any of this?* Who knows?

Ok, but if I did die, what would happen to my family, my loved ones? How would they feel, cope? How would they get along? It would be incredibly hard, but my family would figure it out. And they would eventually move on. It's a tough pill to swallow, but it's true.

We don't know what's on the other side of death, when all of our earthly responsibilities drop away. We may not remember anything, or we may. We may also have the ability to assist and connect from the other side. I know this sounds bizarre, but I don't want to filter anything in this exercise.

This practice also assists me in my storytelling. In an effort to dig deep into my characters' personalities, specifically the protagonist's, I ask similar questions. If I want them to appear three dimensional and display growth, I must put them through the ringer, in the worst possible scenarios. What's the worst thing I can do to these characters? What are their deepest fears? Their choices in the face of these massive challenges reveal character. Over and over, I ask myself, *And then what? And then what?* And when the character faces adversity and overcomes it, as challenging as it was, there is a realization they had the power the entire time; they just had to have faith and trust in it.

When you do this exercise and trace your surface fears back to your *core* fears, the roots of your anxiety, things tend to settle down and become clear. A new reality opens up, and you see things from a different angle. The worst thing that can happen, that one thing you drum up in your imagination, usually doesn't happen.

Once I stripped away everything, I realized I wasn't really scared of death itself, I was scared of never being truly validated, or loved, or feeling complete in this present lifetime. I was scared I wouldn't accomplish everything I want to accomplish *before* I died. And that felt like death. Ironically, I was actually scared of living.

That was a huge insight for me. By asking tough questions, my "character" was challenged, and growth and clarity came forth, all of which instilled trust. And now that it's in front of me, I can align my minutes, my hours, my days, and my years working on purging this sense of lack, understanding it more in an effort to free myself from these life chains, and focusing more on my journey and not the destination. There is so much beauty right in front of me. And there is so much accomplishment already within me.

You are a character in this film called life, and the challenges you face, consciously and courageously, cause you to become a more well-rounded and complete individual.

Your biggest fears, when you really focus on them, tease them out, get some perspective, aren't really that bad at all. The Stoics practiced negative visualizations, imagining worst-case scenarios vividly until they could take the power out of them. Besides, who knows, death might be magical, a new beginning. And then what?

DON'T WAIT
FOR THE CALM

It may never come.

Seriously.

At least, not the way you expect it.

An astrologer once told me that I had "diving-board syndrome." What that metaphorically meant was I'd get to the end of the board, look down at the water, think of all the reasons not to jump, and then turn around and walk away from the edge. I'd then repeat the process over and over, getting more and more caught up in my negative mind stream. I was waiting for the inner calm.

Jumping in when things are *not* internally calm can be unbelievably frightening. But when you do, when you step into the fire, *when you feel the fear but do it anyway*, you shake up your system, short-circuiting it, creating a seed of inner courage that boosts your self-esteem and, ultimately, creates calm.

If you don't take a leap of faith, if you stand at the end of the board frozen, looking down at the water, you'll only strengthen that nasty fear.

I don't care what it is you are facing: an important conversation, a business meeting, a new job, a labor of love, getting married, having children, traveling, whatever.

Don't wait for everything to be perfectly lined up, physically or emotionally.

Jump in.

It's scary. I get it. But if you wait for the calm, your whole life might pass you by.

Have you ever gotten the advice, "Do the opposite of what you feel"? What this means is "do the opposite of what your body and emotions are telling you to do."

Obviously, there are times your internal alarms should not be ignored.

But since everything in this book is framed for individuals who struggle with anxiety, I'll tell you, those alarms are frequently false.

More often than not, we avoid interactions and experiences by convincing ourselves they won't be good or safe for us.

"Wow, I'm really feeling on edge, maybe it's not a good idea to go out and meet friends tonight or try this new thing. Yup, not a good idea, I'll go when I feel better, more like myself."

You've just fed the demon.

At the same time, deep down inside, there is a little voice saying, "You're full of shit. You are perfectly fine, and you are avoiding this because you are a scared, little bitch. "Not the nicest way to speak to yourself, but if you are dialed-in, really observing, aware, you'll know it's wise to listen to this voice.

One evening about sixteen years ago, I had a lot of resistance to going to a filmmaker event in Los Angeles. I had so many excuses and fears, not the least of which was my reluctance to interact with other people and my general sense of shame about where I was in my career compared to where I wanted to be.

I went back and forth on that diving board. *Should I or shouldn't I go?*

I ended up attending, and that night, I met my future wife.

You *are* yourself at all times. So don't wait for calm and peace, ever. Push yourself. Challenge yourself. Relish the idea of anxiety as an opportunity to practice. Nine out of ten times, when you do, you will see how much these life experiences open you up to new possibilities, people, and positive transformations.

Take a deep breath, and jump.

ACTUALLY, YOU SHOULD ASK FOR MORE ANXIETY, FEAR, AND PANIC!

IN THE PAST, EACH AND EVERY TIME I'VE HAD HIGH ANXIETY OR TREMEN-
dous fear, I believed it was evidence something really horrible was about
to happen. Even though these feelings were tied to an experience I'd been
through a zillion times, it didn't matter. I thought, This *time, I just may
not make it through this unbearable pain.* This *time, I'm done.* My heart was
going to give out or my brain was going to short circuit.

I have had numerous fears and concerns I've dealt with over the years, and
to this day, they have *never* come to fruition. Or if they have, they have
never arrived with the intensity and complexity I envisioned.

- Health scares

- Relationship scares

- Career scares

- Finance scares

All that worrying and obsessing for nothing. Wasted time.

Two of the most sought-after psychotherapists in Hollywood, Phil Stutz and Barry Michels, wrote a book titled *The Tools*. The second tool they share is Reversal of Desire. They explain, "Pain avoidance is a powerful habit. You get immediate relief when you defer something painful. The cost—helpless regret at a life wasted—won't come until far in the future. This is why most people can't move forward and live life to the fullest... Focus on the pain you're avoiding; see it appear in front of you as a cloud. Silently scream, 'Bring it on!' to demand the pain; you want it because it has great value."[37] You picture the worst-case scenario and convince yourself you actually desire it and love all the wonderful pain involved. Your mind doesn't know how to deal with this new behavior, and what happens is the pain and fear eventually retreat.

I am sure you've had more than a handful of high-anxiety and fearful days in your life. Many of those days have been filled with full-blown panic where you thought you just may die.

You've made it through those rough waters over and over again, and you will continue to do so in the future. That is my point. *Nothing* happened.

Let me repeat that: *nothing happened.*

So if you enter a situation where all your internal alarms begin to flash and blare, notice it, lean into it, invite it, sit with it, and feel its expression in your body. This isn't a method of creating more pain in your life, it's taking the pain that you face on a daily basis and flipping its power on its head. Using this strategy of inviting your fears can be very powerful. So, what if you took it a step further and relished those moments of utter terror? Say, "Bring it on! I see you! And I welcome you! You are not real, you don't own me, and you will vanish in time!" If you take a chance, you'll see that, in the end, you will be fine. You'll actually be transformed, even if ever so slightly.

This is the "I see you, Mara" moment. Who is Mara? He represents afflictions of the mind. In Buddhism, Mara is the demon who had a major battle with Buddha the night before his enlightenment. Mara tempted the meditating Buddha as he sat under the Bodhi Tree with his beautiful daughters and armies of monsters. The story goes that Buddha sat quietly and touched his hand to the ground, which then shook violently, and Mara disappeared. Buddha woke up the next day enlightened.

Telling this demon that we notice him, we are *aware* of him, is all we need.

Tara Brach suggested in her book *Radical Acceptance* that Buddha eventually invited Mara to tea and treated him as an honored guest. Buddha offered Mara a cushion so he could sit comfortably. He filled two earthen cups with tea, placed them on the low table between them, and only then took his own seat. Mara stayed for a while and then went, but throughout, the Buddha remained free and undisturbed.

The reason Mara left is because the Buddha invited the mental noise, honored it, and, at the same time, remained focused, compassionate, and calm.

I know this is easier said than done, and it may be wise to have a skilled anxiety therapist hold your hand as you navigate these rough waters, but I'm telling you, if on some level you want to conquer your anxiety demons, you need to open your arms, smile, and welcome all that nasty shit in. Give it a shot. Start with the small triggers and fears. Invite your demons to tea. Demand it. They may just transform into paper tigers.

SHRINK THE HEAD

In my mid-teens, I was swimming in unknown deep, dark waters. I was beyond fearful and sad. I say that now looking back, but at the time, I had no idea what I was feeling. The only discernment I had with emotions was they either felt good or felt bad. I certainly didn't know why I felt a certain way. I know now I didn't have any information about these things called "anxiety" and "sadness" back then. I had no tools. I had no one to explain my emotions to me. And that only exacerbated my anxieties.

I was certain something was terribly wrong with me.

I had no one to turn to. I felt completely unsafe bringing any of my feelings to my mother or father. I felt shame. And I was too proud to bring my struggles to any of my friends.

Admitting I needed help was unbelievably tough. I fought it until I could not fight any longer.

So I picked up the phone in my college dorm room, an actual landline, and called a psychiatrist. I vaguely remember finding his number in a phone book. Yes, a phone book.

The only previous experience I ever had with a mental-health professional was when I was in elementary school. My mother and father took me to a child psychologist because I was getting in quite a bit of trouble. I was told to draw a picture of anything I wanted.

I drew an airplane...crashing.

This was a recurring dream for me. Usually, I was watching from a distance. This was strange at the time because I really liked airplanes. I thought maybe I would be a pilot one day. Plane-crash nightmares, coincidentally, are generated by minds that are trying to process fearful emotions. The founder of modern psychology, Sigmund Freud, believed plane-crash dreams represent worries, anxieties, and loss of control in our waking lives. Bingo!

The advice the psychologist gave my parents? No more soft drinks. I was hyperactive.

I felt, subtly, even at that young age, that I had done something horribly wrong and my parents were not happy with me. Worse, I felt something was wrong with me. That I just may be broken. The seed had been planted.

Something *was* wrong. These were clear symptoms of trauma, and this psychologist completely missed the telltale signs. And then misdiagnosed me.

I also understand the risky and mischievous behavior I engaged in was all an effort to feel truly alive, something I struggled with as I had long ago disconnected from my body in order to protect myself from perceived danger.

The hardest part wasn't the call I made to the psychiatrist, it was actually going to see him, actually walking into his office. Over and over, I thought about what my father would think, what my college buddies would think. I was terribly conflicted.

Once I sat down in the psychiatrist's office, he began to ask me very specific questions. I answered and elaborated on what I was experiencing. He then diagnosed me, which happened in a very short period of time. I felt so much relief.

He took all my fears, insecurities, and obsessions and "shrank" them down to a very simple explanation: a DSM disorder. An anxiety disorder.

Under any other circumstance, I would have been devastated hearing I had a disorder. My mind would have a field day with this, further crushing my already-low self-esteem. But in light of the fact that a professional had now provided me with two words that explained everything I was feeling, my first reaction was optimism and, dare I say, joy.

I now know it's not that simple. A diagnosis is one thing; a treatment plan is another. My shrink's conclusion was a bit off, and his prescription regimen was excessive. After all, he was looking at the symptoms, *not* the cause.

However, he put me on a path to recovery. He listened to me. He validated me. He put me at ease.

He made me aware that I didn't have to live with this pain alone. He actually recommended I attend group therapy, but, at that time, I figured, if the medication worked, why would I need therapy?

When I called my father soon after my first session, excited, knowing I was actually ok and things would be getting better but also fearful of how he would react, he was confused and upset. He said, "Why did you go to a psychiatrist? You're fine."

My father was right. Now that I had been given this diagnosis, I was *fine*. Or, at least, better. I now knew this thing I struggled with was real, and it was treatable.

I believe my father was struggling with the idea his family may not be perfect and this imperfection, his son's psychological issues, may just be a reflection of him and his skills as a father. He was correct in his thinking.

This single visit started a domino effect that led me on a journey of self-exploration that continues to this day.

I believe in psychiatry and therapy...as a starting point. It's a wonderful jumping-off spot, a place to get some clarity, to uncover your core issues. But you must be careful because it can become a crutch. Seek out help, work your main issues, then move on and figure out things, life, for yourself. Ultimately, you are your own best therapist.

NIP IT IN THE... UNEASINESS

BEFORE I WENT TO THERAPY, I WAS LOST. I DIDN'T KNOW HOW MY MIND, body, and deep, unexpressed emotions worked, and I definitely didn't know how they colluded with each other. Most of the time, the early warning signs of encroaching anxiety and panic are very subtle, undetectable, and can present as physical, emotional, or mental signs and signals. Therefore, it *feels* like the anxiety is coming out of nowhere. It hits us hard and fast. But after further exploration, you realize it is not. You just may not be tuned into those very faint signals.

At first, figuring out what sparked an episode, the initial trigger, would take weeks—or longer—but it would eventually come to me.

As I began to "do the work," I found after a blowup, an upset, or just some generalized anxiety I could sort of pinpoint the source, the inflection point, that led to the anxiety or panic attack. As I got more in tune with myself, the epiphanies came more quickly, within days or hours. Now, they come to me in the middle of the struggles, in real time, and I am able to steer myself into smoother waters quickly.

My goal? To pinpoint subtle mental disturbances *before* they escalate to upset, fear, and, ultimately, full-blown anxiety, to stamp out the seed of anxiety before it blossoms. This is definitely a skill, but it is a skill that can be honed. As you come to understand the machinations of your mind more intimately, you will be able to effectively transform the way it works.

I want to be clear: what you are *not* doing here is saying to yourself, "That thing in the *future* is going to cause me anxiety, so I am just going to avoid it." That is *not* nipping it in the uneasiness. That is avoidance. I am also not talking about tracing back to that double-shot latte you had an hour ago or the fight you had with your spouse or child ten minutes ago. Those are obvious trigger points, but we need to go deeper.

My guess is something was brewing. You were already on edge before that caffeine hit or before you dropped that F-bomb on your family member or spouse. These were effects of the anxiety, not the causes. Maybe you grabbed that latte because something was bothering you, the bud of your anxiety was already forming, and as much as we know caffeine can trigger anxiety, we do it anyway, maybe to nurture that bud. Yup, crazy, I know. But damn it, anxiety is what we know, and it feels comfortably uncomfortable.

You are trying to trace back to the initial, probably imperceptible twinge of anxiety. What was that first signal? It was probably something that happened way before you thought about that future event or the event that happened in the recent past. Once you learn to recognize that bud of uneasiness in real time—maybe even before, when it's a seed—you can nip it.

This is deep. This is an excavation. It takes a lot of focus and stillness. Meditation is a great place to uncover the early stages of an unsettled mind. We aren't going for certainty here. We are searching for clues, signposts, to unlock mysteries.

As I've said over and over, you are most likely reliving and responding to a negative event that happened when you were very young.

One thing *is* certain. If you practice uncovering these inflection points, you will really start to understand how this "stuff" operates within you—how your emotional past, mind, and, in turn, thoughts dictate your life.

If you can nip these things early on, you can drastically reduce, or possibly completely short circuit, your anxiety.

NOT KNOWING—HOW TO MAKE UNCERTAINTY YOUR FRIEND

I CAN'T TELL YOU HOW MUCH UNCERTAINTY I HAD WRITING THIS BOOK. Many times, I thought, *Who the fuck am I to give advice? Will people trash it? Is it the same old stuff written in every other book about anxiety? Is it deep enough? Smart enough? Different enough? Am I wasting my time? Will I ever finish it?* This questioning makes me feel terrible. And if I let my mind run too far with it, my next thought may be *Fuck this shit, I'm not doing it.* So in order to stop the madness in its tracks, I choose to accept the uncertainty and continue to move forward. *Fuck you, I most certainly am going to write this book.*

You've heard the saying that the only thing certain in life is change. And maybe that's a good thing because certainty also breeds boredom. That is for certain. Humans do need uncertainty, but they want to be certain about their uncertainties. That's why we go to movies, why we love watching sports, and why we skydive, gamble, and engage in all sorts of risky behavior. We know, for the most part, we will be ok when these events are over. But the uncertainty, the ups and downs in the interim, is a rush.

Uncertainty is everywhere. If you get right down to it, dissect each second in life, every moment is uncertain.

Uncertainty is the foundation of anxiety. So, if we can befriend it and know that it is everywhere and will always be that way, anxiety begins to melt away. It is depleted of its fuel.

You may *think* you can predict the next moment, and sometimes, you can, but ultimately, the only thing somewhat certain is the past, the parts of your life that have been lived and concretized. Even then, it's just your memory and perception of what happened. You really can't be *absolutely* certain.

We don't even know if we will wake up in the morning. (We really don't.) We don't know if our autonomous nervous system will suddenly *not* be autonomous. But we trust it, right? We lie down at night, go to sleep for eight hours, and trust that everything will be ok, that we will continue to breathe, our heart will continue to beat, and we will greet the morning sun. That is immense trust. When we drive on the road, we trust millions of other drivers will keep their cars in the correct lanes and apply the brakes when they are supposed to. That's a lot of uncertainty we are willing to live with. There are actually many things we don't know about life and the future, but somehow, we have faith all will be well.

The majority of uncertainties in life—and really, the biggest ones—you accept, and you get on with it. So, pat yourself on the back. Good job. You already have the ability to accept uncertainty. You have faith. You trust.

Uncertainty is actually the real magic of life.

When I first began writing screenplays, I'd start without an outline, a treatment, or character bios. I had a general idea in my head about these things, and I knew where I was headed, but whoa, I really had no idea where each story would take me.

It was intuitive, frightening, *and* exhilarating. Look, I knew my computer wasn't going to explode in my face and I wouldn't be swept away by a massive tidal wave from the nearby Pacific Ocean, and I also knew that after multiple drafts, I would be in good shape, with a cohesive story that fired on all cylinders. But what I experienced writing those first drafts was a roller-coaster ride—lots of uncertainty peppered with touches of certainty.

My process is a bit different now, as I am always trying to find ways to be more efficient and effective. But there is always plenty of uncertainty.

BONUS: The fly-by-the-seat-of-my-pants, intuitive method always produced wonderful material.

Ironically, what I am aiming for constantly as a screenwriter is to keep the viewer off balance and uncertain in order to create tension, uneasiness, and a vast array of experiences and emotions and provide them with the certain uncertainty they crave.

I also use another writing process as a way to deal with the many uncertainties in my life—journaling. It allows me to shine a light on those dark recesses of my mind that exacerbate the unsteadiness of uncertainty.

Where we start to get in trouble is when we selectively choose our uncertainties to feed our particular anxious patterns. To keep us small, stuck, and scared.

Will he or she like me?

Is he or she going to leave me?

Will I want a divorce in the future? Will my significant other want the same but sooner?

Am I going to get fired?

Am I going to make a fool out of myself in front of everyone?

Will I have enough money to retire?

I am not minimizing these concerns or suggesting you should never have these thoughts, I am just saying they pale in comparison to the uncertainties we just let slide every day. For most of us, these are not life-or-death situations, even though they may feel that way. That is good news. We already know how to live with some *major* uncertainties. So, it's time to learn how to live with your particular uncertainties *and* move forward.

What are your uncertainties? What are your beliefs about them? What keeps you up at night? Can you allow more of them into your life? Can you strengthen your faith, your trust in the process, and at the same time weaken your anxiety reflex? Can you get more comfortable with the certainty of uncertainty?

BELIEFS AND THOUGHTS ARE *REAL BUT NOT TRUE*

I CAN'T TELL YOU HOW MANY TIMES I'VE RUMINATED ON THINGS THAT ARE blatantly not true (and will most likely never be true) over the years. I'm talking ruminating for days, over and over, like someone was taking a drill bit with the nastiest thoughts embedded in it and drilling it into my head. As the bit spun, the centrifugal force shot those thoughts off into the deep recesses of my mind, where they could fester and grow.

One time, I thought I was suffering from some sort of terminal illness, and I was certain death was imminent. Well, I'm still here. There were thousands of times I thought I was going to pass out, hit the ground, and crack my skull open. To this day, I have not fainted once. And there were all the times I figured I was going to lose my mind and check out of reality. Nope. Didn't happen.

Beliefs and thoughts being "real but not true" is a phrase coined by Tibetan teacher Tsoknyi Rinpoche. Question your beliefs and thoughts all the time, especially when you are not feeling emotionally well. Is this belief actually true? Can I prove it beyond a shadow of a doubt? If you recall, this is a tenet of this book. You must dissect and understand your thoughts and beliefs.

Much psychological suffering is caused by a misperception of reality, likely rooted in some sort of childhood trauma. In essence, you are resisting reality because you are not seeing it as it actually is.

See how crazy this is? You fear something, run from something, that doesn't exist at all.

Ask yourself at any moment, "What am I believing right now?" What do you find? You may find you are asking yourself really bad questions, questions that beg for answers that stoke more negativity. Stuff like, "Why do I feel so bad?" or, "Why do I *always* feel like this?" When you ask those negative questions, your mind will answer with, "Because you always feel bad, loser," or, "Because you have an incurable mental disease." Consider instead empowering questions like, "What am I feeling right now?" or, "Is there a pattern to these feelings? A pattern I can subvert?"

You must understand that the flip side is also true, that the good thoughts or beliefs you have also need to be questioned and investigated. In the film business, it is frequently said regarding critics, "If you're not going to believe the bad reviews, you cannot believe the good ones either." You see, the good thoughts are being generated by the same problematic mind. So you can't say, "Well even though my mind is generating all this crap, I'm going to believe this wonderful stuff over here because it suits me."

Of course, it's better to have good thoughts. However, many people don't scrutinize their positive thoughts. Do they match reality? Most of us can look at a very real, very screwed-up situation and be in complete denial about it, kind of like my perceptions and thoughts about my mother's struggles with alcohol. In my first therapy session, I told my therapist, "Sure, she drinks a bit." That was very far from the reality of the situation. My mother was a raging, fall-down, blackout alcoholic. You need to question *all* your thoughts and beliefs.

I'll repeat this idea again: everything you experience is being filtered through your conditioned mind and life experiences. If those past experiences involved chaos, stress, anxiety, and panic, guess what? Any new experiences that are similar will likely trigger those same feelings, even if chaos and its buddies aren't present.

So, you ask, if I don't have certainty about any of my thoughts or beliefs, how do I know where I stand with anything? How do I move forward in life? What do I grab on to? Who am I?

Well, you are reading this book because you suffer from anxiety and panic. So, remember the Cornell study? Conservatively, 90 percent of the time, those fears and worries running through your head are a bunch of bullcrap. *That* you can trust. *That* you can grab on to. The majority of thoughts in your head are false. Negativity bias is primal and hard wired into our system. According to Prakhar Verma, the National Science Foundation found that the average person has about twelve thousand to sixty thousand thoughts per day. Of those, 80 percent are negative, and 95 percent are repetitive thoughts.[38] This automatic process is exacerbated by learned behavior from your childhood, which was most likely accidentally instilled by someone else, usually primary caregivers or people you looked up to.

There is a difference between functional thoughts and conditioned thoughts. Functional thoughts are things that *are* actually helpful. These are usually thoughts that allow us to move through life and take care of our basic needs. And they are generated by the other 10 percent of our mind space.

Your beliefs and thoughts are extremely powerful. And they feel so real. They are the basis for how you see everything. Let's revisit the mantra attributed to Gandhi:

Your beliefs become your thoughts.

Your thoughts become your words.

Your words become your actions.

Your actions become your habits.

Your habits become your values.

Your values become your destiny.

Eventually, you will notice the difference between thoughts from the obsessive, destructive conditioned mind and thoughts from the deep, intuitive functional mind. You will learn to respond instead of react. I know it sounds bizarre to *not* trust your mind, but it is absolutely necessary in order to break free from the chains of internal lies, anxiety, and stress.

IT'S NOT THE ANXIETY, IT'S HOW YOU RESPOND TO THE ANXIETY

WHATEVER STORM IS BREWING INSIDE OF US IS JUST THAT: A STORM. LIKE all storms, it will pass. Usually, after it does, the air feels cleaner, and the sky is clearer. It's the judgment of the storm while we are in it that wreaks havoc.

Alan Wallace, American author and expert on Tibetan Buddhism, offers an interesting analogy regarding thoughts. He says the U.S. Centers for Disease Control and Prevention houses some of the most dangerous diseases in the world. But inside their vials, the otherwise-deadly pathogens are inert and harmless. It's only when they come into contact with oxygen and animals or humans that they become unbelievably harmful. By keeping them contained behind glass, scientists can safely observe and learn from these diseases without getting ill.

Similarly, negative thoughts (and their accompanying anxieties) are empty, inert. It's our resistance, our judgment, that gives these thoughts oxygen and weaponizes them. It would be better to simply examine them in the vial, the vacillating mind stream, to see them for what they are—just thoughts, neither good nor bad—from a safe and objective distance. And then watch them dissipate. Instead, we usually go, "STOP! GET OUT OF MY FUCKING HEAD, NOW!"

Do you think the trees, the grass, the plants, or the flowers curse at storms? The amazing storms that ultimately bring them water and nourishment and allow them to grow?

Most people freak out in the face of their internal storms. They may grab a drink. Others may reach for a joint or bong. A lot of people work too much, watch porn, or pop a Xanax, Ativan, Lunesta, or Ambien. And all of this may provide temporary relief or escape, but in the end, it usually exacerbates the issue, creating more anxiety and turmoil. For me, for many years, I never gave myself the chance to move through the fear or painful experiences. I distracted myself with everything imaginable. Mostly, I would keep busy multitasking. My to-do list was always a great starting point because it was never ending. If not that, internet wormholes were always there for me, awaiting my lack of focus, procrastination, and fear. I would fill every single second of my day with something to do. Busy felt like I was making progress, even though, most of the time, I wasn't. In the past, stillness and presence or simply slowing down would fire up my fearful and abusive mind. *You're a lazy piece of shit, you don't deserve to relax, you'll never get to where you want to go unless you are constantly moving forward.*

So, I was in constant motion. The dark feelings would retreat momentarily, but since the deep, old programming hadn't been worked through and out of my system properly, its ugliness returned as soon as I became still or even just slowed down a bit.

When the high wears off, when the busyness subsides, when the oxytocin and endorphins work their way through your brain or the benzos leave your system, guess what? You're right back where you started. The underlying pain, the cause, is still there. And it will continue to be there until you face it.

And worse, more often than not, you develop a tolerance to the busyness, to your drug of choice, so you require more of it to ward off your mental demons. They will continue to get louder until you sit up, pay attention, and observe them without judgment.

What if we were to look at the tightness in our chest, our clammy hands, the out-of-body experience and say, "Wow, I'm feeling really anxious right now. I know it will pass. It always does. But man, this is intense. I have felt this in the past, numerous times, and I have always survived. I am in no danger right now. What is this anxiety trying to tell me right now? Can I pause and listen intently?"

I learned this firsthand. I would respond, not react, then wade deeper and deeper into the uncomfortable pool of my feelings. At first, I only submerged myself up to my ankles, but eventually, I'd wade in up to my neck, staying with whatever came up until I was able to dance and *sit* with my deepest, darkest thoughts, emotions, and fears:

- This pain will never end.

- I'm dying.

- I'm losing my mind.

- I may hurt someone.

Moment to moment, over and over again, these thoughts would confront me, reminding me I wasn't done yet. I still had work to do.

I do my best to stay with the funk, observe it, feel it, and let it move through and out of my body instead of analyzing and reacting harshly to it. In that process, I'm sure there will be, at the very least, a kernel of wisdom that will give me some insight into where this pain is coming from and what I should do next. It doesn't necessarily come to me in the moment, either. Sometimes, it comes to me on a walk later that day.

You don't need to dredge up all your negative childhood experiences and chart them out on graphs. It may be as simple as sitting with "the pain" in a non-judgmental way until it works its way through your system and dissolves. I know it's painful, and it sucks, *but* from my experience, after three decades of it, it's really the *only* path to release and peace.

You will eventually have a realization that the pain and suffering you are experiencing is exacerbated by your resistance to what is.

As Hamlet said, "Why, then 'tis none for you; for there is nothing either good or bad, but thinking makes it so."[39] So you see, it's not the anxiety, it's our negative thoughts and reactions to it that make it the horrible thing that it is.

Greek Stoic philosopher Epictetus said, "What upsets people is not things themselves but their judgments about the things."[40]

Everything in our life is subjective, including our perceptions and the meaning we give to things.

Meaning #1: This is horrible, and I am going to die. Probably in the next few minutes.

Meaning #2: I am feeling intense emotion. Wow, this must be what it's like to live life deeply and fully embodied. I'm gonna ride this wave for a bit and see where it takes me. What can I learn from this?

Stress and anxiety are really just energies coursing through our bodies. Instead of observing them, feeling them, and letting them untangle and release, which would provide relief and peace, we tend to fight them.

Hey, I know this is all easier said than done. It takes practice. It's like building any new habit. What initially seems like an affirmation will eventually become a new belief.

It will take baby steps. *Newborn* steps. Patience. Sometimes, it will feel like you are moving backward. That's ok. The path to peace and calm is not about instant gratification. The backslide can be informative in its own unique way.

It can be done. You have to have faith and trust. The more you view your situation from a different angle, respond to it instead of react, and lean into the pain and uncertainty, the more things will shift.

The more and more you show up with courage in the face of perceived danger from an objective place and understand you have a choice in how you respond, the more things will subside and work out, and you will start to trust yourself and your ability to weather any anxiety superstorm.

KNOW IT...LIKE A STOIC

I HAVE ALWAYS BEEN DRAWN TO THE TEACHINGS AND PHILOSOPHIES OF THE ancient Greeks, possibly because I was raised Greek Orthodox, and I love going back to my roots. That, and I love storytelling and drama.

In the past couple years, I have been particularly interested in the teachings of the Greek and Roman Stoic philosophers. Thousands of years ago, before Sigmund Freud, Charles Darwin, and, yes, Oprah Winfrey, famous Stoics like Seneca the Younger, Marcus Aurelius, and Epictetus were developing the inspiration for the modern study of psychology.

In a nutshell, Stoicism claims a happy life will come about if we are present, in the moment, and not swayed by the pains or the pleasures of life.

Live in the moment and don't let outside—or inside—forces determine your well-being. Sound familiar?

In the past, the Stoics got a bad rap or were misinterpreted. Some thought following their tenets would create withdrawn, unfeeling, grim, humorless, emotionally flat-lined, inert individuals.

Friedrich Nietzsche went after the Stoics in his book *Beyond Good and Evil*, stating that they were surrendering to a life of indifference. He said,

"You desire to *live* 'according to Nature'? Oh, you noble Stoics, what fraud of words! Imagine to yourselves a being like Nature, boundlessly extravagant, boundlessly indifferent, without purpose or consideration, without pity or justice, at once fruitful and barren and uncertain: imagine to yourselves *indifference* as a power—how *could* you live in accordance with such indifference?"[41]

Today, Stoicism has made a big comeback, infiltrating the self-help world, and the criticism has shifted to the idea that the ancient philosophy has been bastardized and simplified; a sort of Stoicism-lite that cherry picks the easier practices of the Stoics and ignores the philosophy's basic underpinnings.

Really? Who gives a fuck? If something works, it works. I only hope you cherry pick what works for you from this book.

Stoicism is not about indifference. It's about equanimity. Bestselling American author and Buddhist teacher, peacemaker, and activist Jack Kornfield states, "The near enemy of equanimity is indifference or callousness. We may appear serene if we say, 'I'm not attached. It doesn't matter what happens anyway, because it's all transitory.' We feel a certain peaceful relief because we withdraw from experience and from the energies of life. But indifference is based on fear. True equanimity is not a withdrawal; it is a balanced engagement with all aspects of life. It is opening to the whole of life with composure and ease of mind, accepting the beautiful and terrifying nature of all things. Equanimity embraces the loved and the unloved, the agreeable and the disagreeable, the pleasure and pain."[42]

Stoicism is not about the suppression of emotions. It is about knowing them— all of them—feeling them fully, and, with regard to negative emotions, learning how to defuse their control over you by not fighting them.

Author Ryan Holiday states, "Obstacles make us emotional, but the only way we'll survive or overcome them is by keeping those emotions in check—if we can keep steady no matter what happens, no matter how much external events may fluctuate...It's the kind of calm equanimity that comes with the absence of irrational or extreme emotions. Not the loss of feeling altogether, just the loss of the harmful, unhelpful kind. Don't let the negativity in, don't let those emotions even get started. Just say: 'No, thank you. I can't afford to panic.'"[43]

In the *HuffPost* article "What Stoicism Isn't," professor of philosophy and author William B. Irvine states, "It wasn't *emotion* that the Stoics were opposed to; it was *negative emotions*, such as anger, anxiety, jealousy, and fear. They had nothing against positive emotions such as delight and even joy."[44]

As with any philosophy, you don't want it to become dogma. I think the negative assessments of Stoicism treat it as such.

True equanimity is similar to the idea of surrender. This doesn't mean you throw your hands in the air and give up; it means you accept what is and then figure out a way to dance with this-is-ness. Move forward while accepting the outcome, moment to moment.

I suggest picking up anything from Epictetus, Seneca the Younger, or Marcus Aurelius. Their philosophies and teachings are a wonderful addition to any anxiety sufferer's toolbox. Cherry pick from them all!

EXTRICATE THE CRAZY FROM YOUR LIFE

We all have people in our lives who drive us crazy. Teacher, author, and artist Julia Cameron described these individuals as "crazymakers" in her book *The Artist's Way*.

She wrote, "One of the things that we do when we are blocked creatively is that we get involved in intense codependent relationships. We seem to pick people who are absolutely expert at turning the tables on our creativity. Crazymakers discount your reality. Crazymakers are expert blamers. Crazymakers create drama, but seldom where it belongs. Crazymakers hate order."[45]

For me, my main crazymaker is my older sister. She's struggled with mental illness for many years. The seeds of her emotional struggles were apparent when she was very young. We were never terribly close. We lived together for a short while when I moved to Los Angeles, but her mood swings and behavior associated with her mania and eating disorder became too much for me to handle. After I expressed my concern about her downward spiral and she told me in so many words to fuck off, I promptly moved out.

My sister had her first methamphetamine-induced psychotic break in 2003, just before my father died. I had warned my father of my sister's downward spiral. I actually told him he needed to come out to LA immediately. I was worried my sister may not be alive for much longer. He waffled. Since I lived near my sister and my parents were on the East Coast, I became the go-to helper, the pseudo-replacement parent. I really resented the fact I was being put in a position to care for my sister. Where the fuck were my parents?

Since her mental and emotional breakdown and multiple severe diagnoses, she has been in and out of hospitals, board-and-care facilities, and assisted-living homes. More than a few times, she ended up on the streets of LA. When my father died, I had no choice but to care for her. Or I at least *thought* I had no choice. Part of me was like, *She's my blood, and I need to look after her.* That's what you're supposed to do for your family. I became her conservator and caregiver. Naturally, my anxiety skyrocketed. I found it unbelievably hard to care for my sister and love her at the same time. To separate the person from the illness.

Because I signed on as my sister's conservator, I was forced to take full financial responsibility for her about four separate times over the years. I had to act in her best interest even when *she* wasn't acting in her own best interest. She nearly burned a condo complex to the ground and was later picked up by the Santa Monica police after she was found strolling the streets naked and out of touch. When my wife and I went to remove her items from her condo, we found burned books in the oven and excrement covering her bathroom walls. To make matters worse, I had to deal with a mental-health system in Los Angeles that is inept and complicated. Navigating it was incredibly hard for me and on me. More than a few times, I thought my sister and those closest to her would be better off if she were dead. I feel deep shame saying that, but it is true.

A few years after my father died, the crazymaking multiplied when my mother became helpless and her addictive demons resurfaced. This was her remedy for her depression and anxiety associated with tremendous loss. Truth be told, I think my father's death opened the floodgates to the pain my mother felt around the loss of connection with her daughter. Truth *really* be told, this all spawned from emotional issues born in her own childhood. With echoes of my father saying, "Take care of your mother" banging around in my head, my mother essentially became my responsibility as well. It was a shit show.

The day my wife and I returned from our New Orleans wedding in a state of bliss—a wedding both my mother and sister attended—a Bethesda Chase Rescue Squad volunteer contacted me. He proceeded to tell me they had to break in to my mother's home to attend to her after she fell down the stairs in a drunken haze. Not to be forgotten or upstaged, my mother had brought the attention back to herself in grand fashion. Bliss became horror.

Who knows if this was a conscious or unconscious act. Did she feel like she was losing me? It didn't matter. I later found out her binge began in New Orleans, where she first wiped out the mini-bar in her hotel room and then continued at the wedding. There was so much going on, I just hadn't noticed. Or maybe I was, once again, in denial.

I believe on some level my wife and I did not have children because we were essentially already raising two. It's not that my mother or sister were doing anything wrong. They were struggling with mental illness, and they were being mentally ill. However, I had the choice of whether I wanted to engage with this madness or not.

I let both of them suck the life out of me with their constant phone calls, texts, demands, guilt trips, and, yes, death threats. In some strange way, I did feel needed. By taking care of their constant needs, I felt like I was getting shit done and being of service. And that felt good. And since it did, I put up with their verbal attacks, victim mentality, and psychosis. I also put up with constant fear, uncertainty, and shame. As my mental health began to deteriorate, I realized I needed to make a big change.

I now put myself and my wife, *my* family, first. I have very firm boundaries with both my mother and my sister, which, to this day, are constantly tested. I have put a social worker between my sister and I, hired a care manager for my mother, and continually confront the both of them if I feel they've crossed a boundary. I've put autonomous systems in place. I need to do this to maintain some order, some sanity. Otherwise, I would never be able to support either of them. I still struggle when engaging with them, and pangs of guilt still surface here and there, but I do my best. In a sense, I have extricated the crazy by shielding myself from their destructive vortex. I love them from a distance.

Another firewall I installed was moving my mother from her home of thirty-plus years to an independent-living facility as well as finding her a very good psychiatrist. Her withdrawal from the world into a small bedroom inside a 3,500-square-foot home was increasingly putting pressure on me, as she lived three thousand miles away and relied on me for everything. After I moved her, she spiraled into painkiller abuse, severe depression, and anxiety. She pretty much recreated the situation from her home in a new location. It was the worst I'd ever experienced with her. At that point, I cut off all communication. I trusted she was safe and getting the assistance she needed, and if an emergency arose, the facility or her psychiatrist would contact me. Months went by, and slowly but surely, my mother started to heal, and she started to take some responsibility. What I realized was enabling her negative behavior only made the situation worse. Extricating the crazy not only helps you, it forces the individual wreaking havoc in your life to be accountable for their choices, for better or worse.

My anxiety around the relationships with my mother and sister has lessened substantially, even though both of their situations have unfortunately worsened. My sister presently calls a hospital her home, and my mother, now with round-the-clock care, has not left her bedroom in months. She refuses to shower or take care of her everyday needs and will most likely need to be transferred to a higher level of care. And as sad as that is, I know it was her choices that brought her to this point, and there's nothing I can do to stop that. Obviously, my situation is an extreme example. But I believe minimal interaction and clearly defined boundaries can make your crazymaker—jobs, life situations, and experiences—less "crazymaking."

When designing a story or screenplay, a common practice is to make the majority of the supporting characters diametrically opposed to the main character's goal. And I don't mean a small opposition; I mean major, constant opposition. Many of these characters would fall into the "crazymaking" category. This is to create drama and conflict, challenge the main character, and force them to grow. The choices the characters make as a result of these conflicts and uncomfortable situations reveal depth, personality, and motivations.

Look at your life very closely. I bet many of your interactions have an element of "crazymaking" within them. Who in your life is challenging you constantly, and not in a good way? What choices are you making? What choices are you *not* making? And don't forget, we are essentially the number-one crazymakers in our own lives, as we delude ourselves with wild thoughts, beliefs, and perceptions.

You see, in order to keep our anxiety, stress, and panic alive (remember, we feel safe when it's around), we need to set up our world so that some sort of anxiety-provoking thing is right around the corner at all times. I think that's probably the main reason I kept putting myself in the situations I did with my family. These "crazymakers" allow you to continue to feel your anxiety. Because if you didn't feel it, something would be wrong, right? For me, I also felt needed and important and confused this with love.

There is a pattern of self-sabotage that goes on to keep you feeling certain and comfortable. And to you and me, that comfort zone is anxiety. So, keep a keen eye out for these troublemakers. Remember, it starts within us. Be mindful of the crazy shit you tell yourself. You may need to cut ties with individuals who have been in your life for a long time. Maybe even best friends. This may feel unsettling, like you are losing control, because they've been such a huge part of your life design, a design to keep you anxious and stuck. Eventually, you will feel it in your gut. You'll know if you are butting up against something you need to engage with and lean into *or* it's just a "crazymaking" situation or individual, and you need to draw a very firm boundary.

BACK END OF THE SPIRAL

When I graduated from college, I was feeling pretty good. I was proud that, despite my struggles, I completed my undergraduate studies with respectable grades and received my bachelor of science degree in communications. I had found love after a string of unsuccessful relationships and stopped my medication regimen, and I had big plans for the next steps in my life. I knew I wanted to tell stories. I wanted to be a screenwriter, a filmmaker. I tentatively and temporarily moved back into my parents' home and applied to graduate film school.

This home was a major source of my anxiety and held a lot of painful memories for me: experiencing my first panic attacks, feeling utterly alone, and witnessing the massive emotional disconnect between my mother and father. Up until the day I moved my mother out of this home and sold it, I felt a lot of resistance when returning there to visit. After a little less than a year living there, I was accepted to the master's film program at American University in Washington, D.C. Suddenly, it all went to shit again, and my fear and anxiety came roaring back. At a time when I thought I should be elated, I was locked in fear.

I was right back in the shoes of that seventeen-year-old just finishing high school and entering college, swallowing a severe panic attack in the back of a car near Dewey Beach. The self-talk, negative thoughts, and horrible physical feelings blew open like a dormant volcano. I was certain I wouldn't be able to survive in grad school, not feeling like this. I believed everything I'd done up to this point to ward off my symptoms was all done in vain. I felt like I'd taken two thousand steps backward.

Even today, because of my ability to feel at a much deeper level, I experience anxious episodes that rock me more than the ones I felt when I was younger. My initial reaction is to see these experiences as setbacks. I say to myself, "I am getting worse, right? Not better. I've wasted so much time. This will never end." Now that I have more perspective, clarity, and awareness, I realize how wrong that thinking is. Welcome to the back end of the spiral.

At that time, I wasn't really conscious of the subtle inner work I had been doing. But the little things I had begun practicing before college, like meditation or the simple realization that something was off, the awareness, were laying the groundwork for my recovery. Furthermore, going to see a psychiatrist, receiving a "diagnosis," and getting more knowledgeable about anxiety and panic attacks allowed me to feel more resilient in the face of it.

Imagine a spiral that spans from the ground to the heavens, like a staircase. Sometimes, the spiral gets narrower; sometimes, it grows larger. It's an upward, circular funnel. As we move through our lives, as we learn, grow, and work through challenges, we move in a circular motion up the spiral.

Now imagine the front end of the spiral, the visible part, is all the wonderful feelings, emotions, and experiences we have on our journey. And the backside, the part we cannot see, is sadness, anxiety, depression, panic, and darkness.

What if we determine any successive bout with anxiety is a huge setback or, even worse, we believe that nothing has changed and our recovery is a complete sham, that nothing has shifted. Well, this just isn't possible.

Once you've reached a certain height on the spiral, you cannot descend. You cannot unlearn things or erase experiences. You actually continue to build on what you know.

So, those perceived devastating setbacks? Well, you are at the back end of the spiral. It may feel like you are at the bottom because as you rise, the back end can actually feel more intense than the ones you experienced at a lower level. You will also realize your ability to feel a lot more joy in your life, which will paradoxically expose you to even deeper levels of pain and sadness.

As more observations and awareness come into the picture, all emotions and feelings get amplified. But you are right where you need to be, with all the tools, insights, and healings you've collected along the way. So don't obsess about it. You are not back to where you started. It's not possible. It never will be. Rejoice.

RUMI-NATION

I HAVE STRUGGLED WITH RELENTLESS, OBSESSIVE THOUGHTS MY ENTIRE life. Abusive, fearful, scared-to-tell-anyone-what-they-are-because-they-are-really-fucked-up kind of thoughts that have kept me small, worried, and full of shame. These aren't just unwanted thoughts; these are unbelievably loud, intrusive, repeating thoughts that will do just about anything to grab my attention. Groundhog thoughts.

And I am not specifically speaking about the content of the thoughts. I am speaking about the relentless energy underneath them continually pushing these unwanted thoughts into my headspace to be noticed, to be believed, to be ingrained. There have been times I actually thought I just may be possessed.

I've tried to *stop* these thoughts. I've shouted at them. I've taunted them, and yes, I've even ignored them. Sometimes, this works, but it's usually a short-term fix.

And the rumination continues.

The first thing to remember is these thoughts are not accurate. As real as they feel, you can disregard the content right off the bat. The fact that the thoughts are so loud and repetitive is the key sign that they must not be trusted. Relief, right? To put it simply, you are in a trance.

The second and even more important thing to remember is to let the thoughts—and that insane energy underneath them—be. Let me be clear, ignoring and letting them be are two different practices. Letting be is not a practice at all. It's as if you are watching a ticker tape pass by, not rejecting or judging, not grasping, not analyzing, not doing anything but observing. Maybe even laughing at the ridiculousness of it all. Don't grasp at a solution. The solution is to do…nothing.

There is a quote attributed to Rumi, a thirteenth-century Persian poet, Islamic scholar, and Sufi mystic, that says: "Only from the heart can you touch the sky." This was the quote my wife and I placed on our wedding invitations. It says heart, *not* mind. Ruminate on that.

Another quote attributed to Rumi is: "Put your thoughts to sleep, do not let them cast a shadow over the moon of your heart. Let go of thinking." In both quotes, we see the importance of letting our heart shine and be the source of our wisdom, be the one to guide us, and help us avoid giving in to the incessant chatter that infiltrates our mind and, in turn, our lives. Maybe instead of willing peace and calm, doing nothing about these thoughts is the answer. I know it is hard and doesn't completely make sense, but that's because you are trying to solve this equation with your mind.

Like dealing with a child throwing a tantrum, I find it best to just let these thoughts burn themselves out and finally give up. And let peace return of its own accord.

DESIRING AND WAITING FOR PEACE, JOY, BLISS, NIRVANA

MY WHOLE LIFE, I'VE WANTED PEACE. TO FEEL SOME DAMN RELIEF FROM the constant and reckless abuse emanating from my own mind. If it wasn't telling me to prepare for a heart attack, cancer, or impending doom, it was screaming at me, "You are and always will be a failure!" The scary thing is, when I was younger, I was not aware of it. I thought this was all normal and all these messages were the truth and needed to be acted upon.

Just before I entered college, when I started on my spiritual journey, my goal was to feel more peaceful, joyous, and comfortable in my own skin. At the time, I didn't understand the difference between religion and spirituality. Even though I grew up Greek Orthodox, I didn't completely *get* religion. It felt manufactured, superficial, and not deep or profound. It seemed like most people, including my family, were showing up to church every Sunday out of guilt, not to listen to the sermons, take the advice, understand life and their place in it, or strive to be better people, but to show off their new cars and beautiful children, flaunt their wealth, or quell their superstitions of what would happen if they didn't attend regularly. I came to realize this path was not going to take me where I wanted or needed to go.

As I began to grow spiritually by practicing the most basic meditations, seeking professional help, and becoming more conscious of my internal process, new ideas began to form. I thought I was gathering the tools I needed to quell these horrible feelings. And I was, but that was *all* I was doing. I was trying to manage it, keep it at bay. When you live a life of anxiety, panic, and sadness for many years, you want the alternative quickly. But looking back, I realize grasping for what I perceived as positive feelings or mental states didn't do me any good either. At least, not entirely.

If I constantly had my eye on achieving joy, peace, and enlightenment, I was resisting the present moment. And as horrible as that present moment might have felt, it was where I needed to be. Otherwise, I was missing out on what the painful feelings were trying to tell me, not the least of which was that I needed to look directly at them and feel them if I wanted any sort of relief. Not feeling them and processing them was delaying my trip to "nirvana." And that is exactly what happened.

Maybe happiness is overrated. First of all, if we didn't have deep suffering, we wouldn't know the peaks of joy *or* happiness. It just wouldn't be possible. You actually need a little pain, fear, and anxiety in your life for well-being, for spice, for seasoning. A dash here and a pinch there.

Us humans are led to believe if we are not happy and content most of the time, something is wrong with us. In reality, something is not wrong with you.

Move into and engage with the experience life has brought you. What do you have to lose? You may just be on the precipice of a breakthrough.

You see, because you are resisting ugly feelings created by this ugly place in your life, with your eye on some utopian future, you are creating a gap. And that gap is where suffering, stress, and anxiety take hold.

I realized that, as I wanted and waited, ignoring the present, all the bits of beautiful and amazing that were right before me were never appreciated. As Irish-American actor, writer, and politician Malachy Gerard McCourt purportedly put it, "I had one foot in my past, one in my future, and I was pissing on the present. My life was passing me by."

I still struggle with this. There is part of me that frequently wants anything other than what I am experiencing in the present moment. It's a delicate dance of striving for peace and doing the deep work while also staying present. I must remind myself of this over and over in order to bring myself back to what is, right now. I feel gratitude knowing I have the wisdom to do this. And that gives me peace. You have the ability to do it too. Start with a daily routine.

DAILY "SPIRITUAL" PRACTICE

WHAT CAN YOU DO EVERY DAY TO TAKE A SMALL STEP FORWARD?

In order to tame this beast we call anxiety, panic, or stress, you *must* have some sort of daily practice. This has nothing to do with religion. I call it "spiritual" because it nurtures my spirit. You can call it whatever you want. You must show up every day ready to dance with Mara.

Remember Mara, the demon that tempted Buddha by trying to seduce him with the vision of beautiful women? Instead, Buddha meditated under the Bodhi Tree for forty-nine days straight without moving before his enlightenment.

Buddha showed up every day no matter what, and regardless of what was thrown at him, he sat still, unperturbed.

You must be committed. You must do something different than you've been doing, become a different person than you've been in the past, for change to occur. Before you get all concerned about the time this might take away from surfing the web or numbing out on TV, realize you will start small. Remember, newborn steps. Just do it. Just do something. Chip away every day. *Every* day.

Find your go-tos. Personally, I try to *sit* seven days a week. By sit, I mean meditate. Sometimes, twice a day. This allows me to ground in my body, still the mind, and observe my thoughts from a distance, as a witness. Sometimes, these thoughts will produce insights; however, a lot of the time, it's a thick stream of painful worries, concerns, and fears. And I just let them be. Before I sit, I will usually begin with a few rounds of deep breathwork or an uplifting read or YouTube video. I also regularly train with weights, run, mountain bike, and periodically do yoga. Sometimes, all that energy that has built up inside us has absolutely nowhere to go, and no amount of surrender will do. Moving your body can do wonders and set you up to reclaim your sanity. The trick is to find something you enjoy that is effective. Make it a daily practice.

Some other things I enjoy plugging into my day that ward off daily stress and anxiety:

- Sitting until inspired. Literally. I sit, eyes open, relaxed, in silence until I am moved to do something.

- Do-nothing breaks. This is not meditation; it literally is doing nothing. And it's harder than it seems.

- Slow down in order to speed up.

- Do something that scares me.

- Hydrate. I shoot for about eighty ounces of water a day. A half an ounce to an ounce for every pound of body weight.

- Laugh.

- Write/journal. This has been very eye-opening for me. Some people write freehand, but I usually make entries into my calendar program on my computer. That way, I can do a simple search and see my progress. Most importantly, I can see where I was stuck, what was going on in my life at that time, what season it was, who I was engaging with, etc. I don't do this every day, but I do it enough to allow me to see patterns, which assists in tweaking what isn't working for me.

This may all seem insignificant, but these seeds planted have the potential to make very large changes down the road. We brush our teeth every day, right?

We will dig into a more elaborate plan later in this book, but for now, the key is to just start, and start small. Maybe a few steps out of your comfort zone. Don't beat yourself up if you miss a day, or a week. Just pick up where you left off. According to the wisdom attributed to the Stoic philosopher Epictetus, "Progress is not achieved by luck or accident, but by working on yourself daily."

YOUR COMFORT ZONE IS KEEPING YOU UNCOMFORTABLE

AFTER I HAD "MANAGED" MY ANXIETY FOR MANY YEARS, IT RAMPED BACK up with a vengeance. It was pretty much saying, "Time to deal with this shit you've been putting off and managing for years once and for all." It kept creeping in more and more until my comfort zone got so small, I didn't feel 100 percent safe in my house or my bedroom. And that led to feeling unsafe in my own body. Yes, I became extremely uncomfortable in my comfort zone.

I developed slight agoraphobia and claustrophobia. It was sometimes hard for me to embrace my wife under the sheets before we went to bed. I felt hot and trapped, and I wasn't able to lie still. Fear and anxiety would bubble up in me, and I had to tear off the sheets, separate from her, and be by myself. My fear of going insane was debilitating. This all made my world incredibly small. A comfort zone is meant to be expanded. However, anxiety wants you to live in this zone forever.

My Sikh mentor Guru Singh told me, "Safety is in the eye of the beholder. Challenging your comfort zone is a requirement." So unfortunately, our perceptions frequently determine what we believe to be safe and dangerous. And for the anxiety challenged, there is a lot to fear in this world. In knowing that, we can confidently test the boundaries of our perceived comfort.

"Eat a death cookie." This is another phrase coined by Hollywood psychiatrist Phil Stutz. He says, "When an action has the tag on it 'extreme fear,' it likely has the greatest value. Pursue it with vigor."[46] It is the process of leaning into these uncomfortable sensations that will take the charge out of the fear. It doesn't have to be a big thing. It can be a conversation you've been avoiding, or standing up for yourself, or doing something you've never done before.

I now strive to push against the boundary of my comfort zone. Ideally, I try to go just beyond it. My edge. When I do, I expand my comfort zone. A circle that is just a bit bigger. I started small, maybe putting my latest creative project out to the world, or initiating a conversation when I normally would not have.

Each time you push against your comfort zone, you will experience fear and anxiety, maybe more than you ever felt before. But the key is to know that as you sit with it and metabolize the discomfort, your zone gets bigger. *You* get stronger. Your ability to know yourself and what you are capable of deepens. Again, each of us has a different comfort zone, triggers, and so on. You need to search yours out like a detective. Then challenge them.

You've been built a certain way, but that doesn't mean you can't do some serious remodeling.

Sometimes, this circle will retract, shrink, and you'll need to push through the old boundaries once again to reestablish the larger zone.

As your zone continues to grow, your anxiety and fear will lessen in situations you used to struggle with. Now, as fear or anxiety arises, it will be a sign you have reached the edge of your newly established comfort zone, and that is a good thing. You may want to test it or pull back and revisit it another day.

Get *out* of your comfort zone because it's only creating discomfort.

ACT 3

THE RESOLUTION: Let Go

BE OUT OF CONTROL

I REMEMBER A TIME IN MY EARLY TEENS WHEN I WAS FULL OF ABANDON, like a just-lit match. My hormones were raging, and I had no concerns about the future, no real responsibilities, definitely no concerns about my health, a group of great friends, awesome music, and no real money worries. I didn't have a care in the world, as the world had not imposed its rules, regulations, and responsibilities on me.

I used to curse like a sailor and get in all sorts of trouble. I was often the instigator. Whether it was toilet papering or egging a house, digging into my parents' liquor cabinet, taking my dad's expensive car out for a joyride while slightly under the influence, blowing up mailboxes with quarter sticks of dynamite, or setting up make-out parties in my basement when my parents were out for the night, I led the charge. I would get my friends in trouble too. I had no regrets and didn't look back. Man, it was freeing. I was *present*, in the moment. I was a friend with joy, inspiration, spontaneity, danger, and fun.

As life moved on and responsibilities took over, it became all about managing my life, dialing it back, not offending others, and maintaining control of everything. Throughout my life, I have thought I could be dying from numerous illnesses, worrying constantly, which I now understand logically was an attempt to control the uncontrollable. What is more insane is that

I was trying to control the uncontrollable that didn't even exist. Obviously, I can eat right, get the proper amount of sleep, exercise, and supplement. But ultimately, my health is not really in my control. I do the best and hope for the best.

Control is what most anxiety sufferers are looking for. Because if we can control the outside world, we will ease the sufferings of our inside world, right? We all know where that path leads. Trying to control everything feeds anxiety and tightens your entire physical and emotional being. Whether you want to believe it or not, there is very little you can actually control in this thing called life. Think about that for a minute. It may be scary, but it's the truth.

We all live on this small rock called Earth, which spins at one thousand miles per hour at the equator's surface and moves around the sun at sixty-seven thousand miles per hour in a solar system traveling at five hundred and fourteen thousand miles per hour through a universe so vast it will give you anxiety just trying to comprehend it all. There is a lot going on here.

If you let that sink in, you'll realize that mostly, we *are* out of control. It may look like we have some power over our external world, but we really don't. We have calendars, to-do lists, reminders, alarms, etc., to create the illusion we have some sort of control. Hell, time exists in order for us to make sense of this crazy world.

According to Lincoln Barnett, Albert Einstein stressed this point about time: "Time has no independent existence apart from the order of events by which we measure it."[47]

What you actually need to do is take control of what you can control—yourself, your inside world, your words, your reactions to your thinking and others—in order to then be able to transform the outside world.

Greek Stoic philosopher Epictetus said this about internal and external control, "Happiness and freedom begin with a clear understanding of one principle: Some things are within our control, and some things are not. It is only after you have faced up to this fundamental rule and learned to distinguish between what you can and can't control that inner tranquility and outer effectiveness become possible."[48]

We also use our physical strength, violence, emotions, money, and other things to wield control over something so elusive—situations, circumstances, and others. One thing is certain: change, on every level. One minute you think you've got something handled, and *boom*, you suddenly realize you don't. And then you start asking yourself questions. Usually, the wrong questions.

Sometimes, it's ok to let it all fly. Especially when your normal routine is to hang on for dear life, trying to control everything. Embody your anxiety. Yes, physically become your anxiety. Exaggerate it. *Be with it in all its ugly glory.* Scream, rant, collapse, and grieve like you never have before. You will find it is actually very freeing.

Close your eyes for a minute, and think about all the things you stress about that are completely out of your control. Don't judge them or give them any additional energy. Don't feed them. If you don't, they will self-realize. Let them go. Clear your mind for things that actually matter. Know that no matter how out of control you "feel," you are ok. It also may seem counterintuitive to "let go" to be more peaceful, but give it a try. You can always go back to white-knuckling it whenever you want.

Moment to moment, you simply let go of outcome and of wanting the world and what you feel inside to be any different. At the same time, take steps to bring more peace into your life. It's called "Surrendered Action."

This is a term that Eckhart Tolle discusses in his book *The Power of Now*: "Surrender is perfectly compatible with taking action, initiating change, or achieving goals. But in the surrendered state a totally different energy, a different quality, flows into your doing. Surrender reconnects you with the source-energy of Being, and if your doing is infused with Being, it becomes a joyful celebration of life energy that takes you more deeply into the Now."[49]

This is not a complex process. When you are feeling anxious or an urgency to get busy or whatever, *stop*; let go. Notice what is going on in your body and mind and stay with it. What are you trying so hard to hold onto or control? Don't try to make your situation or mind chatter any different. Do this for a couple minutes. What will eventually happen is you will slowly expand that timeframe, and it will begin to permeate your whole day.

Remember, you've lived one way for so long, it's not easy to turn the eighteen-wheeler around quickly. The bad habit of *thinking* you've been in control for all these years can cause you to freak out once you start to really let go. But you will be ok. Surrendering to the moment or your situation, letting go of control, doesn't mean giving up or being a doormat. Read that again. What you will find is your actions created out of this surrender are much more pure, intentional, and not tied to the ego (on autopilot). It takes a bit of practice, but you can relinquish control and move forward at the same time.

Breathe, and go back to a time when you were so present, so free, so not in your head that fear and anxiety were foreign to you.

Find that out-of-control place you may have reveled in when you were younger, before life told you what was and was not acceptable and what you should be scared of. Embody it, and hold it with the wisdom and respect you've cultivated as an adult.

TO MED
OR NOT TO MED

EFF ALL OF THIS, JUST GIVE ME A PILL. THAT WAS MY STRATEGY EARLY ON because I didn't know there were any other options. To be honest, I didn't want any other options. I wanted the single quickest path to relief from the overwhelming anxiety and panic I was feeling. Popping pills was just too damn easy.

Looking back, I believe the shrink I met in college was a bit irresponsible. He overprescribed me. And I now realize meds are *not* the answer for me. I have been psych-med clean for twenty-five years. I'm saying this because I know many of you who picked up this book may be on meds or are considering them. I am not a psychiatrist, and everyone's situation is very personal, but, from my experience, I don't believe you need them long term. Maybe they're necessary for a select few people for a select period of time but not the majority. Trust me on this.

Taking medication, for most of us, is *not* letting go. It's holding on as tight as you can. Letting go is a practice that requires effort and work. But that tough work will be rewarded and allow our minds, or psyches, to heal organically.

My sister was diagnosed with borderline personality disorder, bipolar disorder, and schizoaffective disorder. *She* needs medication. She is the extreme. Those meds were her savior, her tether to reality. I would also say, sadly, that her initial need developed into full-blown dependence: emotionally, mentally, and physically. Her brain, her neurochemistry, has been permanently altered from these medications, and not in a good way. She does not know a life without them. However, for the rest of us, psych meds are Band-Aids: the path of least resistance.

It's common for many of us to be quick to adopt a medication regimen as soon as an emotional or mental issue crops up, especially for something a bit more intense and out of the ordinary. This is fueled by a broken medical system that tends to focus on the symptoms, not the cause. You may feel better in the short run, but the underlying issues still exist. You will have a momentary sense of calm and peace, but underneath, a storm is brewing.

I've seen it again and again with friends, family members, and loved ones. They jump on the med bandwagon, and when they come off those meds without doing any inner exploration or excavation, they relapse, over and over again. Like *Groundhog Day*, you will be in the exact same spot you were before you started the meds. It's a cycle: anxiety, medication, relief, discontinue medication, anxiety, medication, relief, etc.

Medications, in the long run, may delay your recovery and ultimately make your anxiety and panic worse because they allow you, in an instant, to get relief without doing any of the hard work required to gain real, long-term peace and confidence. Recovery takes time, patience, determination, and some deep internal work. Moreover, the majority of people, including my sister, who become dependent on these medications are terrified to come off them. And this can have devastating effects. According to the National Institute on Drug Abuse, prescription drug deaths in America rose to an all-time high in 2012.[50]

Again, each individual's situation is different and very personal. Only you will know what is right for you. Always, *always* consult your doctor before changing up any medication regimen. Medications may be required to get you through an intense patch or used in combination with psychotherapy. That's fine. Then, when you feel you are in a better place, with the blessing of your psychiatrist, you should do your best to come off them. Your psychiatrist should be on board with this. The best psychiatrists utilize medications as a last resort, *not* as the first line of defense. If this is not the case with your psychiatrist, you may want to consider switching to one who understands the value of medication and when—and when not—to prescribe it.

My hope is you have someone, maybe even a team, who really understands your particular flavor of anxiety and will attack it at the root, not at the leaves. Western medication is an amazing tool but definitely overused. Our bodies and minds are also amazing and incredibly resilient. They can mend themselves if nurtured and steered in the right direction.

This really comes down to trust. As anxiety sufferers, we don't trust anything. That pain in our chest, that compulsive thought, makes us feel our bodies and minds are out of control. So we search for a quick outside source of relief. If we can learn to shift that perspective, do the tough work, and give our minds and bodies the support to heal on their own, we can change our lives dramatically.

SIMPLIFY YOUR FUCKING LIFE—NOW

When you get right down to it, there is so much in our lives—possessions/things, experiences, distractions, and certainly resentments, regrets, greed, and judgments—we don't actually need. My Sikh mentor Guru Singh told me, "We have enough for our needs, but not our greeds."

We use most of these things in an attempt to fill a void. When I feel insecure, anxious, or sad, I'll search the refrigerator, I'll search the internet, I'll get a fear and adrenaline hit from the news, or I'll silently blame and judge others. Some will shop; numb themselves with drugs, alcohol, or porn; or create needless drama in their lives.

Sometimes, I'll drift into some sneakier obsessive-thinking patterns that create mind clutter, take me out of the moment, and definitely complicate my life. Thoughts like, *My life is shit and hasn't really amounted to anything.* I search and search for what I could have done differently. Or I'll think of all the different ways this or that person harmed me in some way. The list is endless, and once I go down this rabbit hole, it takes super awareness to snap out of it.

Bottom line: we distract ourselves, complicate our lives, so we don't have to feel, live, or grow. Seems counterintuitive, right? When I get anxious, I want to speed up, fill the space. What I *need* to do is slow down, trim out all the bullshit, cut the fat, and simplify.

I am so used to these negative feelings and behaviors, the confusion, the perceived impediments. And as bad as they feel, unconsciously, I don't want to change anything because that would be a trip to the unknown. Who would I be without all my stuff, my busyness, my clutter, and my neurosis?

I am always looking for ways to simplify every part of my life. Get rid of everything I don't need. These things could be possessions, relationships, clutter, emails, and certainly negative mind chatter. I try to minimize input in order to maximize output. So, what does a simple life look like? What would you be missing out on? Surprisingly, not much.

Simplify your life, and live smarter, not harder.

A brain detox is a great place to start. First, you'll need to cut out a few inputs. Or, at the least, drastically minimize them.

Input 1: The news and media. The news is driven by ratings. How do they get ratings? Most often, breaking news. More often, breaking *bad* news. And that bad news, just like bad food or annoying sounds, colors our inner lives and creates anxiety.

Now, I'm not saying you shouldn't be informed. Look, if something is big and important, that info will get to you somehow, most likely through a family member or a friend. Trust me, this news will find you. Certain movies and television shows can also give rise to stress, anxiety, and even panic. Be very selective about what you watch, especially when you feel on edge and vulnerable.

Input 2: The internet and social media. This has to be one of the most anxiety-provoking tools on the planet. It fosters comparison, judgement, envy, procrastination, worry, fear, and on and on and on. A 2017 five-thou-sand-person study referenced in the *American Journal of Epidemiology* found that higher social media use correlated with self-reported declines in mental and physical health and life satisfaction.[51]

We have the keys to the world on our smartphones, which can be over-whelming and an onslaught to our systems.

Input 3: Your home. Your space. What does it look like? Your outer world is usually a reflection of your inner world. So, cluttered space = cluttered mind. This was huge for me. Get rid of stuff you don't need. Start small, a little bit at a time. And this also applies to electronic clutter, like the desk-top of your computer!

Rid your life of clutter and complexities, and it will change dramatically. I am constantly looking at areas of my life to see if there is room for more simplification, more efficiency, more letting go.

I believe Marcus Aurelius' advice regarding the simple things in life is something to strive for: "Most of what we say and do is not essential. If you can eliminate it, you'll have more time, and more tranquility. Ask yourself at every moment, 'Is this necessary?'"[52] Ponder that for a moment.

TRAUMA RE-LEASE

BEFORE MY FIRST TRAUMA THERAPY SESSION, I COULD FEEL THE FEAR brewing in my system. Usually, this took the form of tightness in my abdomen and chest. I knew that this process would require me to be more vulnerable than I ever had been before, and I didn't like vulnerability. But if I wanted to get at the root of my anxieties, the seeds, I would need to proceed bravely. Within a few short minutes of the session's start, I was bawling. I was shocked at how fast the grief came upon me. I fully surrendered to the intense emotions that usually created so much fear in me. I now know it was because I wasn't engaging my head, my mind, to get to this place of vulnerability.

Trauma lives in the body. And unless we notice it, feel it, give it voice, and ultimately release it, it will keep re-upping its long-term lease on our bodies and our lives. It will wreak havoc. Anxiety sufferers tend to live in their heads, and that is why somatic trauma work is a wonderful modality because it is all about the body. Actually, this sort of work heals the split between the mind and the body. The intellect and imagination, born from the mind, are vital to this process, but us sufferers tend to use the mind to override everything, including bodily sensations and feelings. According to many therapists who treat trauma, a combination of bottom-up (focus on the body) and top-down (focus on the mind) approaches is what is needed here—a reconnection, reciprocity. It's intuitive work that asks your deep unconscious to speak and ask for what it needs to heal. And in that healing, we naturally come back to the body.

I want to be clear that trauma can be as horrible as childhood sexual abuse or as seemingly innocent as someone calling you a horrible name when you were very young. We all have traumas in our history—some big, some small—and everyone will react differently to the events of their lives. Also, dissimilar traumas may have similar symptoms and must be dealt with very differently. We want to unearth the events that may have done considerable damage when we were young, creating trauma that continues to drive the emotional bus. Somatic experiencing, founded by trauma psychotherapist and author Peter Levine, famous for his book *Walking The Tiger: Healing Trauma,* is not a process of figuring things out, but rather, it is a process of creating an environment for magic to happen, feeling one's body intently, seeing where it might be tightening, holding back, and what it is trying to tell you.

I've been through decades of talk therapy. It was unbelievably helpful. It made me understand things and set me on the right path. However, it kept me in my head. I never really dropped into the source of my anxieties and fears. This is the problem I have with talk therapy. I kept spinning my wheels. Session after session, I would come back with a whole bunch of questions. I would engage my therapist from the neck up as all my developmental traumas stayed firmly entrenched below. Furthermore, the constant chatter kept reinvigorating those fears, keeping them fresh and alive.

Trauma therapy is a different animal, or at least, my version of it is. It usually involves me closing my eyes within a few minutes of starting the session, and the therapist will then prime me to look within. And to feel. It's all about feeling. Following that, she will ask me a series of questions that she wants me answer with my intuitive, felt self, not my logical mind. There are then pauses, sometimes for uncomfortably long moments, as I wait for the answers from within. Eventually, they come through images and feelings that sometimes don't make any sense at all to my rational mind. It's a process of reliving a situation, dialoguing with my younger self or my parents, feeling the emotions I never felt as a child because it was not safe to do so, or a combination of all three. Somatic therapy allows my system to purge, reorganize, and integrate. It's very experiential and wild. It was a game-changer for me.

I suggest that, if somatic therapy is something you are interested in, you find a therapist versed in anxiety and trauma work. And then go into it with an open mind. This sort of therapy goes against everything I'd known and trusted. I've always wanted answers immediately, usually from the outside: a step-by-step logical process to get me from point A to point B, not some sort of "ask and you *may* receive" type of arrangement. This logical process was keeping me safe and in my head, keeping me from doing the deep dive necessary. Every time I slip into my head, my therapist will catch me and usher me back into my body. This is key, as my tendency is to run to the head for answers and safety. Again, I am not discounting the importance of the mind here. It's necessary for understanding what the body is telling us. Unfortunately, more often that not, it tends to take the lead and do more damage than good. This sort of work requires a lot of trust and courage. Ultimately, it will help you understand and make peace with those very young parts of yourself that never felt safe, weren't validated and loved, and were deeply wounded. The "stories" you've constructed about who you are, the world, will then disappear, and you will once again be able to feel and love fully yourself and others. You'll trust, laugh, experience more joy, and live confidently.

VISIT THE RABBIT HOLE

PSYCHEDELICS, IF NOT SUPPORTED BY A PROPER MINDSET AND SETTING, can be a crapshoot. I've had some fantastic recreational mind-altering trips where I couldn't stop laughing and felt in complete flow with life itself. I also had a few really horrible ones where I would have done anything to end the misery. I know it may sound strange, but I feel I benefited as much from the negative experiences as the good ones. I learned from them in the same way people learn more from their failures than successes. They were incredibly tough, but I realized coming out the other side, *so am I.*

During a particularly harrowing LSD trip, I took shot after shot of vodka to bring me down from the edge of reality. It didn't work. I then searched my best friend's mother's medicine cabinet for any sort of benzo or barbiturate, anything to ease the fear, the temporary insanity. I was on a misguided mission to escape all those uncomfortable feelings coursing through me.

After the alcohol and prescription drugs had absolutely no dampening effect on the LSD coursing through my brain, when I reached mental exhaustion, I stopped fighting it.

I remember jumping into a pool, dropping down to the bottom of the deep end, and sitting there. The crazy thing is I had no gasp reflex or impetus to return to the surface, almost like I had overridden my basic survival instincts. I felt like I could stay there forever. It was wild and quite scary, but I witnessed the power of my mind. And *my* power to engage with it's content or not. I came out of the water quite shaken, but all was ok. And eventually, I returned to planet Earth.

Some in the therapeutic psychedelic world say, "There is no such thing as a bad trip." The thinking is there is always something to be gleaned from these intense experiences. A "bad" trip, one that is very frightening, confronting, and revealing, will reap rewards, maybe more than a "good" trip. "Trust, Let Go, and Be Open" is a common mantra in this field of work. My belief is that, just like in the non-drug-induced world, mental friction arises when you fight your experience and hold on.

Now, I would take all of this with a grain of salt. Obviously, these very powerful substances must be treated with the utmost care. They could cause, if abused or ingested by someone who is psychologically fragile, some real long-term issues.

Back then, I didn't see or understand the therapeutic benefit of these Schedule 1 drugs. I was in it to see faces melt, time bend, and have a rip-roaringly fun time. (They call it "tripping" for a reason.) These days, we are seeing a huge resurgence of therapies utilizing numerous different "medicines," therapies targeted at healing PTSD, anxiety, depression, and addictions.

I was very curious about this psychedelic renaissance. After a lot of thought and research, I took part in an MDMA-assisted psychotherapy session. MDMA (3,4-Methylenedioxymethamphetamine) was actually used in psychotherapy back in the 1970s but was soon criminalized after it became a popular street drug in the 1980s. The effects include altered sensations, increased energy, increased empathy, and intense pleasure. I must admit, even though I'm still fearful about it, I want to try it again. Not because I had a "good time" but because I got a glimpse of the power it and other substances wield under competent and caring supervision.

The reason I chose MDMA, which is commonly known as "ecstasy" or "molly" and is not really a true psychedelic but does have psychoactive effects, is it was on the subtler end of the spectrum, and there was all sorts of recent research proving its effectiveness in treating PTSD, anxiety, and depression.

I had experimented with MDMA recreationally when I was in college. It actually hadn't been scheduled at the time, so technically, it was legal. The experience was, for the most part, wonderful. Usually, after the initial rush of serotonin and a period of slight nausea, the world became, for lack of a better word, pure *love*. Myself and a whole crew of my college friends in our early twenties, male and female, pupils like basketballs, roamed the campus rubbing each other's bodies; sniffing colognes, perfumes, and any other scents that became irresistible because of the chemical coursing through our systems; and sighing over and over again because everything felt so fucking good. We felt so loose, so connected, so uninhibited, as if the skin on our entire bodies was one big erogenous zone.

Well, that was the whole point. That was the draw of ecstasy and, of course, why it was given its name: the sensation you're on the verge of an orgasm for four-plus hours. However, as much as you've heard about this "love drug" and all the warm and fuzzy feelings it gives you, MDMA-assisted therapy is a whole different animal. For me, the assisted experience was the night to my college experience's day. It was reverent, intentional, and, at least for a bit, quite scary.

First off, the therapeutic drug is 100 percent pure. It's not cut with aspirin, caffeine, or some sort of speed like methamphetamine. Dr. Scott Shannon, who legally incorporated MDMA into his therapy sessions with patients in the '80s and now conducts clinical trials, states, "Molly and ecstasy may contain MDMA, or may not. They may be mixed with other things, they may not…Just because your friend says it's ecstasy doesn't mean it's pharmaceutically-pure MDMA."[53] Moreover, the dosage you are given is usually much larger than what you would normally take recreationally.

The therapeutic goal is to be able to look at your deep-rooted traumas directly from a place of total open-heartedness and shift your feelings and beliefs about those traumas in real time. Since MDMA does an amazing job of opening the heart, it can be quite healing. Dr. Shannon goes on to say, "MDMA quiets down the amygdala—the fear center of the brain—enough that people can actually reason through their experience and understand that they survived it, that it's not an acute issue for them anymore and they're going to be okay...It's more of a loving and supporting therapy process than one of confrontation."[54]

My palms are sweating as I write this, as I had *so* much resistance to this experimental modality. For starters, I was not in a good place. I had just filed a massive lawsuit, my mother was spinning out emotionally and mentally, and I was not happy with the direction of my career. I was in the throes of tremendous anxiety and uncertainty, and I thought, *When I feel better, I will do it*. However, at the same time, I was fascinated with the idea of a therapy that involved a powerful psychoactive substance that could potentially reprogram the mind so drastically and quickly. The gravitational pull was too strong to resist.

My curiosity about this radical therapy began just before I wrote a pilot episode for a television series that was based on an inspired but troubled psychedelic therapist. Soon after completing the script, I went out for some creative feedback from preeminent therapists, doctors, and psychedelic explorers. I wanted to make sure my depiction was aligned with what actually happens in a session. One of the therapists, a leader in psychedelic research, offered to introduce me to someone who actually facilitates these inner journeys, if I was interested in experiencing one firsthand. Of course I was. But I was also very hesitant. I put the idea in my back pocket for a rainy day. I couldn't deny the fact this could be an amazing research opportunity. Eventually, after some inner soul-searching and more inner turmoil, it became much more than that. Screw research, I wanted to crack open my own psyche and heal it, and I needed a bigger tool to do that. I accepted the offer.

The woman who ultimately guided me on my journey convinced me to push on past my continued resistance. She had decades of experience, and from our initial talk sessions, she felt I was ready. She said one session could, for some people, be equated to years of psychotherapy.

I traveled up to her small mind-dojo outside of San Francisco, apparently an area home to more psychedelic guides than anywhere in the U.S., if not the world. In the back of a normal-looking home in a quaint Northern California town was a small, rustic studio. Upon entering, I felt a sense of ease, like I had come home. The place had an old-school bohemian style and made me feel safe. My guide, a woman who I had never met in person before, also had a way about her that allowed me to let my guard down instantly. She was an old soul, soft and inviting, and I knew this work was her life's mission. I was in good hands. I felt safe. After some small talk and instruction, we both sat before a mini altar and lit some sage, and I set an intention. I wanted to uncover any darkness holding me back and be held in a safe container while on this journey. I wanted to let go and allow the medicine to do its work.

One of the core issues with individuals challenged with anxiety is we do not want to let go. This is something you must do, on some level, with these substances. You really don't have a choice. Once you ingest the medicine, you cannot turn back. So it takes a level of commitment. Because my guide wanted me to have a bit of control, she gave me the option of two different MDMA dosages. I chose the lower dose. I swallowed it and then paced.

"Twenty minutes. You should feel the effects of the drug in twenty minutes," she said.

I was incredibly nervous. What would I uncover? Would I freak out? Did I take enough? Did I take too much?

She checked her watch and then guided me over to a bed, laid me down, and turned on some beautiful ambient music.

About twenty minutes in, it hit me, hard. I remembered this feeling from my college experiences. A jolt of energy went from my toes to the tip of my head, like a rush of adrenaline. I gripped the bed so incredibly tight. Initially, I was determined to control my experience. The surge of euphoric energy through my body was intense, and I fought it. I actually fought the good feelings.

I rode the emotional bronco for a good while, not saying much. I couldn't. I was overwhelmed with sensation. And resistance. As the journey continued and I reached the halfway point of the four-plus-hour journey, I softened. Then I felt a deep sense of peace, love, and contentment. I kept saying over and over, "I am so glad I did this. I'm so glad I did this. This feels so good." I felt deep love for my wife, my animals, my life. It was all a colorful swirl of sweetness and lightness. I was being held in a cocoon of warm bliss. I felt a sort of confirmation. I had made the right decision. *I just may be cured of this anxiety today.* But this bliss was short lived. As soon as that thought had entered my mind, I quickly swung back to a space of tremendous fear and worry.

I sweated profusely as I vacillated back and forth between these emotions. My guide comforted me. With a hand on the back of my neck, she massaged it, feeling the sweat, and told me it was normal. She said, "It's ok, you are releasing trauma. This is what you are here for."

The cool thing is this wasn't about processing through words. This was a visceral letting go facilitated by a pharmacological boost in serotonin, dopamine, and noradrenaline. Brad Burge, the Director of Strategic Communications for MAPS (Multidisciplinary Association for Psychedelic Studies) said, "MDMA squeezes previously existing serotonin from the brain, while also causing the release of dopamine (a hormone and neurotransmitter involved in attention and motivation), oxytocin (the 'love hormone,' that quiets the fear center located in the amygdala), prolactin (which stimulates familial bonding), and noradrenaline (which, among other functions, enhances the formation and retrieval of memories). It is precisely this cocktail of effects that makes MDMA so potentially useful for PTSD sufferers."[55]

My vacillation between joy and fear was interesting because it's exactly how I engaged with life. If something felt too good, I would quash it. I would go back to that place that felt comfortable: anxiety and pain.

During the journey, I never dropped into a specific troubling and potentially damaging experience from the past, something that I could face with my heart bursting with compassion and heal. For a big stretch of the journey, I was struggling to get my sea legs on the USS Love Trip.

Another thing that came up for me was a sense that I was doing this all wrong and that I wouldn't get the benefit from the journey because of that. Was I not letting go enough?

That feeling was apropos because it is how I live my life in so many areas, always questioning if I'm doing something right enough, fast enough, slow enough, smart enough, calm enough, clear enough, *enough* enough. The culprit of this thinking is the exact thing I wanted to meet head on. I wanted to understand it and ultimately shift it.

As the drug finally wore off, I recalibrated. My guide provided me with fresh fruit, a dose of 5-HTP to ward off any mild depression created by the depletion of serotonin, and water. She asked me a few times, "Are you ok?"

I suspected I was ok, but my core was shaken. *What the hell did I just do?* I didn't really want to leave, as I felt more comfortable with someone watching over me in this broken, open space. But I left the mind-dojo and headed down to the dramatic Stinson beach. This place is so vast and still. On this day, it was overcast, chilly, and devoid of people, which only added to the dramatic effect. I could smell the saltwater as a light wind whipped across my face. It was as if I was seeing an ocean differently this time around, from a different perspective. And that led me to believe something very dramatic had just happened to me.

I shuffled down a pathway, discombobulated, in a fog, but felt a bit lighter. Being in this undeniably beautiful slice of nature was a wonderful landing spot. I felt safely held.

Since my guide said the next few days and months would be my integration phase, I didn't try to make sense of any of what I was experiencing. I treated it just like I did my anxiety: I just let it be.

It was a true journey that reverberated through my system for quite some time. My guide told me that full integration could possibly take a year, if not longer.

When I returned home, my guide checked in with me, "How are you doing?"

"I had a great sleep and then woke up and had a rough morning again. Big emotions coming up. I remember what you said about the potential for new neural pathways to be formed during integration, so to do things I may normally not do. So I reached out to my wife and had her sit with me through an emotional upheaval. This is something I usually would not do. The bottom line is that I have a lot of fear around feeling those feelings. They feel so much bigger than me. Maybe *that* is what a lot of that fear was about. Journaling as things come up."

She then said, "Be very tender with yourself."

Over and over, the advice was to allow the medicine to do its work on me *and* be kind to myself.

It was clear something shifted within. And as much as my mind wanted to connect the dots, I let it be, knowing the neural reprogramming would continue to do its work and the shifts and answers would come. What I do know now is that strong emotions are terribly scary to me, and when they come up, I get overwhelmed, and it feels like I may be dying. I also know that it's my child self that ran from and bottled up these intense feelings. It was overwhelming and terrifying for that little boy. As an adult, I am fully capable of handling any emotional storm. The worst has already happened.

I was very proud of myself for going on this journey. The fact I jumped in, in the face of a lot of uncertainty and fear, was a huge win for me.

Usually, the protocol is to take three journeys within a three-to-six-month period. I completed my second journey in 2019, three years after my initial experience. It was a long hiatus, but that's what felt right for me and my system.

And my wife came along for her own journey.

Even though I was again fearful of letting go to feel fully, this experience was much softer and deeper. The vacillation between fear and calm was there as the waves of 3,4-Methylenedioxymethamphetamine coursed through my system but to a much lesser extent. I was much more interactive. I talked a lot.

I could clearly see I was going deeper this time.

I was able to see themes and topics about my personal and professional life that I would return to over and over again.

My wife was there when I came in for a landing, and I was there for her. It was very intimate and showed both of us what is possible in regard to connecting and sharing our vulnerabilities, our love.

I am not saying you should or should not experiment with this sort of therapy. What I am saying is it is one more tool at your disposal.

Everyone has trauma on some level, big or small. Psychiatrist, consultant, and author Paul Conti, who did his training at Stanford and Harvard, believes that the majority of addiction, depression, and anxiety is birthed from trauma.

After many years of talk therapy, I felt this sort of visceral, somatic experience would be exactly what I needed. An adjunct to my trauma therapy.

It was. What started as creative research for a television project became something much bigger. Just the exercise of me traveling up north, dropping a pill with someone I barely knew, trusting that person, and letting go was tremendously healing in and of itself.

Your mind and body know how to repair themselves…if you let them.

My belief is the majority of the anxiety I suffer with is a direct result of childhood trauma that was mostly inaccessible to me through normal methods. At the very least, I was able to go deeper more quickly. And most important was the integration phase. You must process the experience with someone after or you will be wasting your time. It's not a panacea, but shining a flashlight on your childhood wounds and then healing them in an intense session from an open-hearted perspective guided by a skilled, loving, and knowledgeable individual can really give you some long-term relief.

Do your homework, and see if taking a "trip" is right for you.

RESILIENCY OF THE MIND AND BODY

SINCE I FIRST STARTED THE SELF-DISCOVERY TREK A HANDFUL OF DECADES ago, I'VE continually studied my behavior, my triggers, my traumas, my ticks, my joys, and my loves.

I've seen a clear shift in the way my brain and mind operate. It was a gradual shift, a dissection of the old core beliefs that were then reframed and rebuilt much better than they were before. I'm a radically different human being. On many levels.

Epigenetics is the theory that our environment and lifestyle can actually affect the function of our genes and holistic healing. Recent studies have shown evidence that how we think and live our lives—what we eat, breathe, watch, and listen to, how we move our bodies—is *more* important than our DNA and genetic patterning in regard to longevity, sickness, and illness. There is a feedback loop that goes something like this: environment → perception → thoughts → gene expression. In an NIH article entitled "Is Longevity Determined by Genetics?" scientists speculate that for the first seven or eight decades, lifestyle is a stronger determinant of health and lifespan than genetics.

Read that again. Tattoo it on your damn arm if you need to. Your lifestyle, which reflects your beliefs, attitudes, and values, is a stronger determinant of your health, mental and physical, and lifespan than your genetics. To be clear, it's not the DNA you are born with that is changed, it is the way the DNA expresses itself. Moreover, the brain and mind are malleable. Director of the Resiliency Center at the University of Utah, Megan Call, states, "We now know that the brain is a highly active and malleable learning machine across a person's lifespan."[56] This is huge for you and me because, for starters, we can create new neural pathways in the brain that foster calm, focus, joy, and love. This phenomenon is called "neuroplasticity," which is the brain's ability to shift and create new neural pathways.

This brain-mind flexibility stays with us until the day we die. Neuropsychologist in the Polytrauma Program at the Washington, D.C., Veterans Administration Medical Center Celeste Campbell states, "From the time the brain begins to develop in utero until the day we die, the connections among the cells in our brains reorganize in response to our changing needs. This dynamic process allows us to learn from and adapt to different experiences."[57]

In addition, the mind directly affects the body. Neuroplasticity and epigenetics work in tandem. Negative emotions and feelings stuck in the body, seeded by trauma, that continue to fuel negative mind patterns can be felt fully then metabolized and off-gassed, creating not only more emotional well being but a system much more able to ward off sickness and injury. So this goes way beyond the body-mind connection of yesteryear. No matter what age we are, we can modify our dated neural connections and create a more robust and healthy physical self. Old humans *can* learn new tricks.

We can learn to keep illness, mental and physical, at bay. And it starts with the mind, what we believe, and how we think. American medical doctor, cardiologist, bestselling author, and founder of the Mind/Body Medical Institute at Massachusetts General Hospital in Boston, Dr. Herbert

Benson, states, "Now we have the evidence-based proof that the mind can heal and it should be added appropriately to drugs and surgeries."[58]

If you did experience some sort of trauma early in your life; or your mother, grandmother, and great grandmother were clinically depressed and now you think, *Oh crap, I've inherited the crazy gene*; or you downloaded a bunch of really shitty software from mom, dad, uncle, older sis, brother, teachers, society, whoever, don't fret. You can overwrite that crap and rewire your circuitry.

The key is consistency. Do something every day that makes you more resilient to stress and anxiety. Many of the simple skills you've been introduced to in this book—meditation, presence, allowing, cognitive behavioral therapy, trauma therapy—can do just that. You may have been given a brain that fosters certain negative mind patterns, but you aren't stuck with it. Think of the power in that.

BIOHACK THE SYSTEM

THIS YEAR, AFTER DOING MY OWN EXTENSIVE RESEARCH ON EPIGENETICS, I took a deep dive into understanding my biology and my genetics and what roles they play in my psychological processes.

What up to this point has been considered the stuff of science fiction and fantasy movies is now a reality.

My experimentation process started with more elaborate blood testing that allowed me to understand my physical risks on a much deeper level. For instance, a lipid test, called an NMR LipoProfile, goes way beyond the three cholesterol markers popular with standard testing. This test can reveal potential heart disease in someone who has wonderful total cholesterol, HDL, and LDL numbers, and vice versa. Then, a good friend of my wife mentioned her amazing discovery revealed through genetic testing, specifically her vitamin B deficiency and how it was affecting her mood and psychology in a negative manner. Essentially, a simple over-the-counter vitamin was able to correct the imbalance, just like an anti-depressant. My wife and I were immediately intrigued and contacted the naturopath my wife's friend had seen. Soon after, we had our DNA genotyped. Having this personal history and genetic information is a priceless window not only into the present state of our physical and emotional health but also our past. What is most exciting is this information gives you the power to alter the future of your health.

A couple of caveats: there is a lot of data you will receive, and it is not smart to try to figure it out on your own. You need a specialist to decipher it for you. Since health anxiety was my thing, I was quite anxious as I awaited my results. When they finally arrived, I was greeted by big, flashing lights on the 23andMe website saying, "Before you click this button, know that you cannot unlearn the data and results you are about to see." Although the data from the genetic tests is absolute, the potential health issues gleaned from this data is not. Moreover, some of the data and results may be misleading. This can send us anxiety-challenged individuals down a dark path if we are not careful. For me, though, I figured when I spit into those sample tubes, I was already waist deep. Why would I back out now? I took a deep breath and clicked.

What did I learn? Among many amazing discoveries, I found out I have a certain gene mutation that not only predisposes me to anxiety but also exacerbates it.

It's called a COMT mutation and needs constant maintenance. In a nutshell, the COMT gene is responsible for breaking down the excitatory neurotransmitters dopamine and norepinephrine. Author and national award-winning psychiatrist Bruce Alan Kehr states, "If your gene has a variable that produces less of the COMT enzyme, (the Met/Met variant) then you're naturally equipped with a surfboard that doesn't quite navigate those big stress-waves as easily. With less of that enzyme, it takes your body longer to rid itself of stress-inducing neurotransmitters, leaving you in a state of imbalance for longer, and creating higher rates of anxiety, ruminating…and PTSD."[59] Because of this mutation, I do not tolerate or recover from stress well, and I am more prone to anxiety and adrenal fatigue. I call it the "crazy gene." Add on top of that childhood trauma and bad messaging from authority figures, and it was clear I was off to a bad start. It's a bummer, *but* knowing what I'm up against, I now have some amazing info about my biology and, in turn, my psychology.

Anxiety has new foes, and they are accessible to all of us for a reasonable price.

The good news is you can combat and eventually rewire your genetics with behavior, diet, and supplementation that supports your neurotransmitters and adrenals. You can actually alter the future of your physical and emotional health. So let go of your old thinking about genes and heredity.

Dr. Rudy Tanzi, professor of neurology at Harvard Medical School and the vice-chair of the Massachusetts General Hospital Neurology Department, says, "Your gene expression is programmed to constantly take care of you by destroying all that tissue you're damaging with junk food, by not getting enough sleep, and so on. Inflammation becomes a way of life. If you take sixty to seventy days to achieve a new habit, rewiring by neuroplasticity, not resisting but proactively rewiring—saying, 'I'm going to do something new'—your genes follow suit."[60]

I'm happy to say I have done this. The power of a few lifestyle changes and basic over-the-counter supplements is remarkable. It's not an exact science, but the continual monitoring of the supplements you take, your blood work, and how you feel will yield tremendous results. It's all about getting a better understanding of your inner workings on a molecular level then figuring out how you can utilize that data to combat and hack the perceived fixed ideas you may have about the brain, the mind, and anxiety.

THE VERY TOUGH, BUT TOTALLY DOABLE, ANXIETY CHALLENGE

You're reading this book because you've most likely been challenged by anxiety for years, maybe decades. Now, with a wealth of knowledge, it's time to use what you've learned and challenge it. Here, you are going to put the lessons and theories from this book to the test in your own life.

I'm going to say right up front this challenge is not for the faint of heart. And I'll also say we anxiety sufferers are all faint-hearted. But look, if I did it, went to battle against this imaginary energetic beast for a year plus, you can too.

SET YOURSELF UP FOR SUCCESS

You'll have the most success with this challenge if you set yourself up to win. First, you need to cut out all those anxiety-provoking things you are already engaging in, probably constantly. Everyone has their "list" of anxiety-provokers and crazymakers.

In my experience, the biggies that need to be excised, or at least minimized, are:

- Recreational drugs (duh!)

- Alcohol

- Caffeine

- Lack of sleep—you need seven to eight hours on a consistent basis

- Googling your anxious symptoms

- News (mostly bad and fear-inducing stuff)

- Movies or books that are depressing, fear-inducing, and intense

- Negative people/family members/crazymakers

- Comparisons between yourself and others

- The many distractions you engage in that allow you to *not* feel

- Medication (but only with the approval of a licensed psychiatrist or medical doctor)

As I'm sure you've noticed, the majority of the list above are external things that trigger anxiety *or* things you may run toward in an effort to quell the anxiety. In reality, they all lead to *more* stress and anxiety.

Ultimately, you want to crush the habitual mind patterns at the center of your challenge. But don't fret. You don't have to remove all of your stress inducers at once. I didn't. Doing so could create unwanted stress and anxiety, the exact things you are trying to get rid of. Moreover, if you did cut everything out at once, you wouldn't be able to figure out what the biggies are for *you,* the ones that create most of your anxiety. You have certain things that trigger you more than others.

Be patient with yourself as you proceed, and understand that this is a learning process. No one, least of all me, expects you to get it "perfect" right out the gate. I didn't. I had stops and starts and took four steps back for every two steps forward as I figured out what worked for me. "Perfection" isn't what will get results in this challenge—but consistency will. You have to keep showing up and be willing to take things one step at a time. This challenge is based on the three tenets that sit at the foundation of this book.

Tenet One

Breathe. When shit comes up, pause and sit with yourself, get present, and let the dust settle. Take another breath. You need to shut down all the inputs and just *be* on a regular basis. You need to do nothing in order to lay the groundwork for something to emerge.

How do you do this? Find a quiet place with no distractions, sit down, close your eyes, and watch your breath for five minutes. If that is too much, take three big breaths in and out. Pause your life, your movement, and, in turn, your mind chatter, if only for a moment.

You must get present to create a space for big changes in your life.

And be nice to yourself. Enjoy this slowing down.

Tenet Two

Next, *observe*. You need to become an alchemist. What are you feeling in your body? Is that feeling giving you any clues as to the source of your anxiety? What is the content of the thoughts streaming through your head? Remember—and this is important—you need to dissect what specifically is creating anxiety in your life.

Do it slowly. In the extraction process above, you will see how each subtraction affects you. Get your thoughts out of your head and in front of you. Write about it. Journal every day. Notice what triggers you, and see what makes you happy and calm. Notice your patterns. Document your findings. Get specific. What really needs to be excised? That specific knowledge is power.

Just as important is asking what are the things that create anxiety but you need to lean into? An anxiety therapist could be very helpful in this process, if you feel comfortable with that, but it's not absolutely necessary. If you get still and quiet enough, you will create space for clarity and deep insight.

This tenet is *really* going to test you. But if you want to be able to move through life calmer, more grounded, more confident, more loving (to yourself and others), and more focused, you need to do the tough work.

Tenet Three

Now, *let go*. Don't want it to be any different. Then let go more.

Let go of old, stuck stuff. Shake up your routine. Simplify. Lean *in*. And, if it makes sense and is approved by your psychiatrist, reduce or eliminate your medications. Watch what happens during the weaning-off process. Write about it.

When you have a desire to speed up (maybe you are running from feelings), slow down. And listen. Feel. Do the opposite of what you normally would do. Put yourself in anxiety-provoking situations, and write about what comes up. Engage in a laughing exercise, or meditate on death and impermanence. Again, journal about it. Notice when your anxieties spike, and write down what was happening at the time. That in itself will show you there isn't something *else* wrong with you.

The practices of *slowing down, breathing, observing,* and *letting go* are simple, but you may find they're difficult to commit to long term. As I mentioned, I did this practice for over a year. If that timeframe feels too challenging or intense, you can scale it back. I suggest a minimum of three months. You'll get the hang of it. And when you start to see progress—and you will—it will inspire you to go deeper.

THREE-MONTH CHALLENGE

First month: *Breathe.* Get still, slow down, and meditate. If that sounds scary, set a few minutes aside every day to be still and connect with your body. Unplug and see what comes up. Practice at least five days a week. I find the morning is the best time to do this.

Second month: Add in *Observe.* Dissect your patterns. I suggest some sort of simple journaling exercise in the morning, where you set intentions, and in the evening, where you review. Take an inventory.

Third month: Add in *Let Go.* Let loose. This may look like accepting each moment as it is or going out on a limb and trying something you've never done before that brings up an unusual amount of fear. It also could be letting go of previous behaviors and habits. I suggest taking baby steps here.

You can break down this system into any timeframe you choose—a week, a month—but I've found three months, or, better, a year, are the most impactful. A long-term, consistent practice will give you *real* insight. And it's more doable than you may think.

THE (TOTALLY DOABLE) YEAR-LONG CHALLENGE

This isn't drastically different from the Three-Month Challenge, but you'll be a bit more rigorous with yourself and your tracking as you go deeper. You will pick up right at month four.

The first thing you'll do is *review* your first three months. What did you learn about yourself and your anxiety? What worked for you? What didn't? Where could you challenge yourself more? Where could you pull back a bit, give yourself a break? Get it down in your journal. This data is priceless. Cut out the practices that legitimately didn't work for you.

Months Four through Six: *Breathe More.* Now it's time to create a more formal space and timeframe for meditation or breathing practice. Ten minutes twice a day would be ideal. This does not have to be fancy, but it needs to be consistent. The goal here is to get out of your head and into your body. But for these months, you will be truly accountable to your practice. You will also keep *Observing* and *Letting Go,* as you've done previously.

After months four through six, *review your journal* and adjust your sails.

Months Seven through Nine: For the first week, take your foot off the gas pedal a bit. You've put in a *lot* of hard work so far. What can you do here to feel tethered to some sort of practice? Maybe go back to your first three-month protocol. After a week, add in *Observe with Intention.* I suggest getting a more objective view of your struggles. Enroll in some psychotherapy sessions or an anxiety support group. Establish ongoing accountability and a feedback loop to make sure the data flow in your head is realistic and healthy.

After months seven through nine, *review your journal* and adjust your sails.

Months Ten through Twelve: Add in *REALLY Let Go.* Lean into your *deepest* fears, the really scary stuff, whether it is heights, speaking in public, or drawing a firm boundary with someone in your life. Maybe a psychedelic journey is in the cards? This also may be a great time to discuss eliminating medications with your psychiatrist. Get out, and do stuff that freaks you out. Your palms sweating yet?

After month twelve, *review your journal* and adjust your sails. And then… *celebrate!*

This year-long timeframe will show you the ebb and flow of your anxieties, the underlying causes, the repetition, and how different seasons affect your biorhythms. You can truly see your downslide into anxious periods and what allowed you to dig yourself out of them from a macro and micro perspective. You will have a boatload of information that shows you exactly how you move through the world. The great thing about putting in a year is it allows you an amount of time to see that all those worries, concerns, and the utter bullshit that flows through your head are exactly that. They're *all in your head.*

What you will have at the end of all of this is *your* operating manual: what makes you tick; what makes you feel stress, anxiety, calm, fulfillment, and joy.

You'll have days where you slip up. You'll drink that cup of coffee or glass of wine; you'll avoid feeling; you'll go down the Facebook or Instagram rabbit hole, comparing your miserable life to someone who seems to have it all, beating yourself up for feeling anxiety or stress. You'll believe every ridiculous thought streaming through your head. You'll completely abandon your practice. Don't worry. It's ok. Remember, it's consistency we are looking for here—one foot in front of the other—not perfection. When you do slip up, put down the whip, and instead, journal about it. What caused you to slip up? How does it affect you? Be kind to yourself.

You will go through cycles, ups and downs, being the observer. In my case, I stumbled. I moved forward. I backpedaled. I had breakthroughs and revelations and then took three big steps backward. Then what did I do? I slowed down, took deep breaths, observed, and let go.

I'm still here, no serious illness killed me, and many of the things I fretted about never came to fruition. Or if they did, they weren't as intense as I predicted them to be, and I handled those moments with great dexterity. I shifted my mindset and, in turn, my reality.

Read that again. I shifted my mindset and, in turn, my reality.

Do I now have all the answers? No.

Did I do it perfectly? No.

Do I still have anxiety? *Yes*. And *no*. It's different.

Do I have a better perspective on how my mind and body work and how that all ties into my anxiety? Absolutely. I have more knowledge. More awareness. A different relationship with anxiety. I have power.

I also have more distance from it all. When the emotional turmoil happens, I don't feel immersed in it. I now position myself just outside of it all, where I can be more objective and, in turn, effective.

I admit this is advanced stuff. If this is your first attempt at proactively engaging your anxiety, you will really need to baby yourself. Remember the most important thing: *don't give in to your anxiety*. Showing up, facing it, dancing with it, these things will help you turn anxiety into fuel and allow you to create a peaceful and more meaningful life. You cannot do this wrong. Let go of your perfectionistic attitude. Let go of the outcome.

As I mentioned early on in this book, if you only come away with one practice that eases your symptoms, consider that a win.

I want to remind you once again of this wonderful quote from Adyashanti. It's everything in a nutshell. "All spiritual practices that are worth doing are practices that either help us to see through whatever we're believing in the moment, or they help us let go of our resistance to what is happening."[61] Even if you aren't spiritual, you can grok this concept. We have many ways to practice that, and you need to find what works for you, but whatever it is, *do it*, consistently. Monitor it so you can build the muscles necessary to step into your fear on an everyday basis.

BREATHE, OBSERVE, AND LET GO

Keep doing your practices, and let go of the outcome. When you feel like crap, keep doing your practices, and let go of the outcome. When you feel doubtful and uncertain, keep doing your practices, and let go of the outcome. When you believe you will *never* feel calm, peaceful, safe, and joyful ever again, definitely keep doing your practices, and let go of the outcome. And most importantly, when you are feeling awesome, like you've conquered your anxiety, like it's gone forever, keep doing your practices, and let go of the outcome.

Look, happiness, peace, and calm are overrated. I know those are the things everyone wants, but if we had no pain, we wouldn't know any of those feelings. There are many answers and insights within those challenging feelings and emotions. The more pain and suffering you are able to sit with, the more capable you will be of feeling the opposite emotions. Kind of cool, huh?

I know many things in this book may sound counterintuitive, even paradoxical, to what you *think* would work. A lot of them are. Only from the position that I am in today can I speak these words with confidence. This thing called anxiety is complex. I want to demystify it for you. I want you to be ok with the uncertainty and not knowing all the answers. I want you to know that, despite its complexity, the way to deal with anxiety is quite simple.

Feeling better is *not* complex. And it won't take forever. You just need to chip away at what keeps you from feeling more secure, confident, and loving to yourself, consistently. Put one foot in front of the other.

If while you practice, you notice you are not getting better, feeling better, and you are not in the small group of individuals who need medication on a regular basis, you are not putting in the work. So keep doing your practices, and let go of the outcome.

Please read that once again. As bad as it feels, it is easier to stay stuck, have certainty, and point the finger at someone or something else. Just *do* the fucking work.

It comes down to my three basic tenets:

- *Breathe* deeply and consistently.

- *Observe* and ask yourself what you are feeling and believing in this moment.

- *Let go* and sit with whatever comes up. And I mean *whatever* comes up.

I can hear it now: "It's not that simple."

Don't try to complicate the matter. Anxiety sufferers like to make it complicated because that process keeps the anxiety alive. I've heard every excuse as to why people don't think they can get better on their own. And the majority of them are bullshit. I know because they've been *my* excuses too.

Some of them include:

- "My brain is wired a certain way. It's irreversible."

- "I have a chemical imbalance that only medication can fix."

- "I've tried everything, and I still feel so anxious."

- "It's just too damn frightening and scary to sit with all these feelings and emotions."

- "I'll do damage to my physical body or mind if I sit with these uncomfortable feelings."

Here's the straight-up truth: you are scared of losing your anxiety. Terrified.

If you do the work, you will see change. A little at first. And then you'll know it works, which will build momentum. And you will then have a strong foundation to build from. Stop asking questions, and just start the process. When you trust the process, the process will reward you.

LIVE ON THE EDGE
OF LIFE'S EXPERIENCES;
FEEL LIFE INTIMATELY

I BELIEVE I AM DRAWN TO MOVIES AND STORYTELLING NOT ONLY BECAUSE of the power of the moving picture and its ability to elicit a vast array of emotions but because when I was young, movies provided me a place to escape and actually feel those emotions deeply in the safety of the darkened theater. Furthermore, when I chose the creative life, I didn't know what I was signing up for. Although I get unbelievable joy from the process of creating, I can also get terribly frustrated, anxious, angry, envious, and ashamed as well.

I frequently look at others who took a more traditional life path, the ones who have a secure job, secure income, and children. Sometimes, I envy what I would consider a more traditional, normal life. This feeling usually crops up when I feel down or defeated. Every day, I must battle my inner critic, the lack of validation, the rejection, the lack of financial gain, and the fact that the majority of my projects are stillborn or lay in limbo. With that said, I know for a fact I would be miserable if I looked back on my life full of regret at the fact I never entered the creative game. I also know I wouldn't be happy with a more traditional life.

Whatever life you choose, would you rather live it from the sidelines, safely, being an observer and not a participant, or on the field, taking whacks, failing, learning, and growing because of the pressure, the uncertainty, and the resistance that life will no doubt throw your way if you properly engage with it? I am a better human because of the path I've chosen and how I have engaged with it. I am more centered and peaceful now because of my journey.

Pain, pressure, and discomfort are the impetus for growth.

Eckhart Tolle put it beautifully when he said, "This world is not designed to make you happy. It is designed to challenge you."[62] Through these upsets, curveballs, and extremely uncomfortable situations, we are forced to take action or suffer. We also tend to take stock of our lives during these moments. If we are never challenged, we simply would not grow.

Some choose not to engage with life. They let life dictate their actions and emotions. I know many people like this. But life is meant to be lived, fully. I want to make sure that when I am on my deathbed, I know I went after my dreams full on and faced down all the demons that crossed my path.

A quote widely attributed to Hunter S. Thompson, American journalist, author, and the founder of gonzo journalism, is, "Life should not be a journey to the grave with the intention of arriving safely in a pretty and well preserved body, but rather to skid in broadside in a cloud of smoke, thoroughly used up, totally worn out, and loudly proclaiming 'Wow! What a Ride!'"

Marcus Aurelius also gave us sage advice: "Think of yourself as dead. You have lived your life. Now take what's left and live it properly."[63] This may be a hard proposition to swallow because you, myself, and many who suffer from anxiety or depression have been pre-programmed to feel life more intensely and more intimately than others.

I'm not talking about the reactions to high-risk activities like jumping out of a perfectly good plane to skydive or running with the bulls in Pamplona. We can feel this intensity from shifts in the wind, sounds, the emotions of others, or walking down the street to the coffee shop, which can then send us into an emotional tailspin. We can feel panic and dread simply laying in our own beds. But we avoid it. Run from it.

Feeling life intimately includes feeling your emotions. Actually, this should be a starting point. If you cannot feel internally, deeply, it will be tough to feel honestly in relation to others and life. And here is the kicker: stuffed emotions cause anxiety. And stuffed emotions are probably the result of trauma, little or big. It's like keeping a lid tight on a pot of boiling water. The energy has nowhere to go.

The more open and vulnerable you are, with yourself, with others, with life, the more you release those repressed demons that just may be creating the anxiety in the first place.

As much as I love going to the movie theater to see a feature, the cover it gives me to feel my emotions, it's not always a pleasurable experience. If the story is deeply dramatic, sad, or intense, I feel waves of anxiety build up in me. When I struggle to fully experience these emotions, I do my best to breathe through them, but there are many times I would prefer to get up and leave. I don't.

Bottom line, you and I are wired differently. If you can fine-tune the highly sensitive antenna that is you, selectively choosing what you will and will not receive, you may just surprise yourself.

I turned my pain, fear, and self-loathing into creativity. I became an artist, a writer/director, which is an outlet for my pent-up emotions. It actually allowed me to start engaging those emotions more often in real life. Maybe that is the real reason my soul called me toward the creative life. I was able to channel all of this wounding and its ramifications into projects that others could learn from. If I can educate someone, provoke them, inspire them, and challenge them through these efforts, my job is done.

Sharing my story was, in part, an effort to face my fears, my anxieties, and my worries then engage and dance with them, channel them, into something that could help others. And to do that, I had to lean deeply into life, my vulnerability, and my traumas and uncover truths I just may not want to face or believe. Go to your edge, and do something that scares you!

Bake a few death cookies.

EPILOGUE:

REALLY LET GO

WANTING TO DIE

I NEVER ATTEMPTED SUICIDE. I HAD FLEETING THOUGHTS AND IDEATION. And those thoughts scared me. They usually surfaced when I didn't have a grasp on my challenge or when I had bouts of nihilism. However, it came more from a place of curiosity. What would it be like to exit this life and not have this insane pain anymore? Tempting. But the uncertainty of death scared me just as much. It became clear that these compulsive thoughts were a result of my OCD.

In my darkest moments, I understood why someone might want to off themself. I got a glimpse of the desperation that may lead someone down this path. I never, not once, thought about taking it a step further. After all, remember, I was scared to die. Health anxiety ruled my life.

As a writer drawn to the dark material found in psychological thrillers, I need to visit these challenging places every now and then. I must draw on my wild, twisted imagination to create the troubled and sometimes homicidal characters that inhabit my stories. When I'm not thinking about ways to off myself or others, I sometimes meditate on the nature of death. I incorporate Buddhist death meditations into my spiritual practice. I visualize myself dying or lying in a coffin. It forces me to face the last stop in life head on, in all its gory detail, right down to the maggots eating away at the inside of my dead body. This is all to, for one thing, lessen my fear around death but also to cultivate presence in my life more fully. Time, life, is ticking by.

Of course, I cannot know how each individual experiences pain and suffering. I am not in the "snap out of it" camp, and I'm in no way trivializing what someone goes through leading up to the decision to take one's own life.

I know many individuals who suffer with debilitating anxiety as well as clinical depression have thought about suicide and that this is a very complex and real thing. For many, there is definitely an issue with brain chemistry. This cannot be discounted. As I've mentioned, I have firsthand experience with family members who would not be able to survive on this planet without medication. With that said, even on medication, the pain can be immense and overwhelming. Suicide should never be the answer to your anxiety struggles.

It *seems* like a simple solution, but that couldn't be further from the truth. The anxiety is not *you*. To kill yourself would be so tragic, as you would be killing off only a very small part of you that isn't really *you* at all. It's that part, that stuck part, that perceives things to be fearful, worrisome, and tragic, tricking you into thinking this feeling, this state, is the entirety of who you are and will always be.

As bad as it feels, feeling that the only thing that would relieve your pain would be to end it all is a case of horribly skewed perception. Take a pause, breathe, reach out to someone you love who loves you back. This will be incredibly hard, especially in the throes of hopelessness and unbearable pain, but it is possible.

Suicide is *never* the answer. It may seem like it is, but it isn't.

Suicide survivor Ken Baldwin spoke of the moment he leapt from the Golden Gate bridge, "I saw my hands leave the bridge. I knew at that moment, that I really, really messed up. Everything could have been better, I could change things. And I was falling. I couldn't change that...It was like your life flashing before your eyes, except it was my current life. It was everybody I was going to hurt: my wife, my daughter, my mom, my dad, my three brothers. I've never felt anything like it, that profound sadness."[64] In another interview, he recalled, "I instantly realized that everything in my life that I'd thought was unfixable was totally fixable—except for having just jumped."[65]

Ken was asked what he would say if he could go back and talk to his twenty-eight-year-old self. He said, "Find a loved one, and believe them when they say that you're worth it. Every single day, I go, 'I get to do this!' And when it's a bad day, I go, 'Ok, I can get through this.'"[66]

You want the anxiety, the pain, and the suffering to die, not you. And that is absolutely possible. So let it all die, immediately, so the fullness of who you are can come forth.

PART OF YOU
WILL DIE

I AM, DECADES LATER, STILL SHEDDING THE PARTS OF MYSELF THAT KEEP me stuck, suffering, and anxious. Writing this book was very confronting, as I knew I would be laying out some of my childhood experiences, core fears, and vulnerabilities for all to see. The part of me that wanted to stay safe, invulnerable, by keeping my story locked away where no one could judge it needed to die.

When I say "die" I am referring to a process, a metamorphosis, that involves communicating and making peace with those parts that are very young and very scared, taking over for those parts, letting them know they are not alone, and feeling the feelings that were not allowed. This requires softness, not aggression. What then happens is a transformation and integration of those wounded parts into something new that thinks and behaves differently, has new beliefs, and allows me to move forward peacefully and confidently. However, this process may *feel* like a battle to the current self, a fight to the death.

Now, on the other side of that debilitating fear, I am a slightly different person. To be honest, shining a light on those parts that held me back, then alchemizing them, like the fearful, wounded child that lives with shame and uncertainty, allowed me to excel in many areas of my life.

As Marcus Aurelius said, "Dig deep; the water—goodness—is down there. And as long as you keep digging, it will keep bubbling up."[67]

It's hard to let aspects of our personality go, even if they are the one thing standing in the way of a deeply fulfilling life. It can feel like cutting off one of your digits; a death. There will be uncertainty, and most likely more anxiety, fear, panic, and a whole host of other crap will come up. I don't say this to scare you but to prepare you.

Anxiety has been your security blanket. Now it's time to let it go. This blanket is made up of many aspects of you that are stuck, most likely in the past, and that are terrified and worried and feel unsafe engaging with the present reality. And they need to "die"—be reframed, in order to give birth to different patterning and behaviors. Cognitive reframing is a method that allows you to shift how you see things, challenging the validity of thoughts and giving different meanings to aspects of yourself.

Know that once these aspects, your neuroses, get wind of their possible demise, they will pull out all the stops in a fight for survival. They will get louder. You will be tested. The egoic or conditioned mind, that part of you buried underneath layer after layer of trauma and misinterpreted life situations, your "security blanket," does not want to change. Because change feels like death to both the wounded child self and the healing adult self. I know that's something you don't want to hear, but it's so vitally important.

Once you bring awareness to these aspects of yourself, call on them to reveal themselves, they will challenge you even *more*. Remember, you must be gentle, let these parts of you know that they are safe and that you will take the wheel now. Thank them for doing their best to protect you, but let them know their job is no longer needed. They can relax. You must know that, as painful as this process is, you are healing, but it may not feel that way. It may feel like things are getting worse. But in order to shift this very young part, you must feel all the pain that the part was unable to feel. This is where most people give up, forget everything they've learned, and stop practicing with their tools. Doing so just feeds back in to the initial problem. This process, honoring and challenging your anxious self, may cause you to feel like you are on the verge of some sort of breakdown. And you are. You are breaking down all the things that no longer work for you, the things that keep you stuck.

This concept is wonderfully exemplified in Christopher Volger's *The Writer's Journey,* which is based on Joseph Campbell's *The Hero with a Thousand Faces,* a common template for all storytelling. Volger speaks of death and resurrection at the climax, or the eleventh stage, of the journey: "Heroes have to undergo a final purging and purification before reentering the Ordinary World. Once more they must change...A new self must be created for a new world."[68]

Just before your rebirth, shifting from pain, anxiety, and suffering into peace, a final and very brutal battle will take place. You must trust that moving toward this uncertainty and fear will abolish the inner discourse from your psyche, bring resolution, and ultimately free you.

As English theologian and historian Thomas Fuller said, "It is always darkest just before the day dawneth."[69]

You may not be ready to slay your "demons" the first time around. You may need to dip your toes into the deep end of your struggle then retreat. Next time, it's up to your ankles, then your waist. Then, you dive. Any of these paths are fine. I've personally tried many different approaches. There have been times I required a slower process. Other times, I'll jump in full bore. Either way, you must meet those parts of you face to face, love them, heal them, integrate them, and in doing so, leave those wounded versions behind for good. That will be hard. Because it will feel like part of you is dying. That part of you has been with you on your journey up to this point. Its mission, albeit misguided, has been to protect you.

But it will be ok.

You will be ok.

Take the leap. And trust that dawn is coming.

ALL OF YOU
WILL DIE

As I write these words, my office is being pounded by a rain we rarely experience in Los Angeles. Lightning lights up the inside walls in short, electrical bursts, and thunder causes them to tremble. This afternoon, it will be over. Most likely, the sun will shine bright. A little death.

This morning, I got the news a family member is dying from Stage IV liver cancer. I wasn't surprised by the news, as this person has been a lifelong addict and chronically abused their body. Still, the news of death, especially when it's a loved one, is always a sobering and difficult process.

When someone close to you is dying, you tend to sit up straight, feel deep sadness and maybe some regret, and possibly even think about your own mortality. I sure did and do every time life whacks me with the truth. I quickly think about the rest of my life on this planet and how I would like to live it.

Death is certain. Death is all around us, happening all the time.

According to the United Nations, about two humans die each second.[70]

Buddhist nun, teacher, and author Pema Chodron says we are dew drops on a blade of grass. Japanese Buddhist priest, writer, poet, and philosopher Dōgen Zenji said, "Form and substance are like the dew on the grass, the fortunes of life like a dart of lightning, emptied in an instant, vanished in a flash."[71] One day, you will no longer exist on the physical plane.

All life is impermanent. Death and rebirth are happening constantly, at every moment. Everything is in flux all the time, including your anxiety, your ups and downs. This concept is so vital, as it will give you the impetus to face your challenges head on. If not now, when?

Facing your fear of death, impermanence, is huge. If you can dance with it, be at peace with it, your everyday anxieties will pale in comparison. The idea that life is actually very short and you will die puts *everything* into perspective, including your anxiety challenges. Start facing your fears now or risk taking them to your grave.

WHERE I'M GOING

(I HOPE YOU COME ALONG)

- *Breathe.* Be present.

- *Observe.* Pay attention to the moment-to-moment feelings in your body, your beliefs, and thoughts.

- *Let Go.* Do not resist life.

I live by these tenets. I constantly check in with myself throughout the day to see if I am doing those three things. Don't try to make it more complicated than that. Your mind will want to, so tell it, "No thanks."

It's been a wild ride, this thing called life. I was so stuck, so terrified, so in doubt, I never thought I would be able to pull myself out of the mental and emotional tailspin I was in. I had no direction and no emotional support system. And I kept on hearing the same things from the beautiful, supportive individuals in my life.

Let go.

Get still.

You will prevail.

I now know my paths, my obstacles, have been there to shape me and teach me. Ryan Holiday's book *The Obstacle Is the Way* exemplifies this beautifully: "The obstacle in the path becomes the path. Never forget, within every obstacle is an opportunity to improve our condition…All great victories, be they in politics, business, art, or seduction, involved resolving vexing problems with a potent cocktail of creativity, focus, and daring. When you have a goal, obstacles are actually teaching you how to get where you want to go—carving you a path."[72]

This is my soul's journey. I'm being called to another level. I believe it is the beginning of the destruction of my ego.

The universe was not happy with the way I was progressing in life. It made this very clear to me, including through life situations that created an intense ramp-up of stress, anxiety, and fear. I needed to expand my beliefs of who I was, what I was capable of doing, and what I was worthy of receiving. I needed to let the intelligence of life flow through me and teach me. It actually *is* on my side, but I never looked at it that way. Don't get me wrong, I still struggle and have really bad days. Now, I welcome the struggle. I don't fight it.

If you are drifting in life, the universe will help you course correct. It will lightly knock on your door in your thirties, bang on it in your forties, and take an axe to it in your fifties.

You and I have the gift of being ultra-sensitive to our minds, bodies, and the world. And with that sensitivity comes anxiety. Many call it a disorder and want to place us in a box with a label. They also want to say it's bad and we must get rid of it in order to lead normal lives. And to do that, you need to jump through hoops, take medication, and sit in a therapist's office for decades. None of that is true. You have *everything* you need inside of you to heal what ails you, including stress, anxiety, and panic. The power is *within*.

You must become a different person, the person you were meant to be, to lessen the fear and anxiety that rattles your nervous system. You must rewrite your story. You must engage with it differently.

You must know that anxiety is constantly waiting for the right moment to strike. That crack, that tiny little space, is all it needs to sneak in and grow like a cancer. It knows you, and it knows your weaknesses. It's relentless. Don't give it more of what it needs, the fuel to keep it alive. Don't fight it. Over and over it will test you, especially if you are trying new things and pushing yourself to grow. Trust me: things will coalesce; they will become clear to you. Use what works, and throw out the rest.

I'm telling you, I've experienced everything this "disorder" has to throw at an individual, and it did *not* win. I am no different from you.

The greatest movies ever end with some sort of catharsis for the main character: a revelation, a breakthrough, a deep understanding. The definition of catharsis, according to the Greeks, is "The purification and purgation of emotions—particularly pity and fear—through art."[73] I *really* relate to this, and you certainly don't have to be an artist to relate. Life is art. We are creating every single moment: ideas, thoughts, new beliefs, relationships, and opportunities.

When all else fails, let go. And go back to presence.

And *love*, first yourself and then others, even if it's just for a moment. Do it. Love yourself. For yourself. And for others.

Keep showing up. Keep facing those perceived demons head on. You are stronger than you think you are.

You are stronger than you will ever understand.

Keep showing up and...

Have faith.

ACKNOWLEDGMENTS

I want to thank:

My wife. Thank you for loving me, accepting me just the way I am, and helping me heal my deepest wounds. You are amazing and have shown me what true love is.

ALL the individuals who helped me navigate the world of anxiety over the years: my doctors, therapists, guides, and the men from my numerous men's groups. Thank you for helping me realize I am not broken or alone.

Steven Pressfield for giving me the inspiration and courage to write a book. And to stand up to the forces of resistance.

My developmental editor, Ann Maynard. Without her, there would be no book—or maybe there would be, but it certainly would not be the polished piece it is today. I am deeply grateful that I found you.

Bethany Davis, my copyeditor, you went beyond the call of duty to help in any way you could. I am incredibly grateful.

Scribe Media for holding my hand through the publishing and marketing process. You made this process enjoyable and exciting. You made my work better.

All the peeps who helped me with beta reads and title feedback: Matt, Tony, and Merabi. As much as I despised this process and feedback, it helped immensely.

Brooks and Steve, my creativity accountability partners. Thank you for keeping me in check and lifting me up when I needed it.

My mom, dad, and sister. I wouldn't be the man I am today if I had not been born into our family. You all had your challenges, and you did your best. And I know you loved me. I am still trying to find compassion and, ultimately, forgiveness for all of you. It's a long process, a tough process, and I'm getting there—one foot in front of the other. This book is part of that healing.

LIFE. You've thrown a lot of crap at me. And you've handed me some beautiful gifts. Keep on bringing it. So I can grow.

ENDNOTES

1 Seneca the Younger, "Letter 90, Paragraph 34," in *The Tao of Seneca: Practical Letters from a Stoic Master: Volume 2*, trans. Richard Mott Gummere (Cambridge: Harvard University Press, 2017), 247.

2 Marcus Aurelius, "Book 9, Paragraph 13," in *Meditations: A New Translation*, trans. Gregory Hays (New York: The Modern Library, 2012), 129, Kindle.

3 Nigel Nicholson, "How Hardwired Is Human Behavior?," *Harvard Business Review*, July–August 1998 issue, https://hbr.org/1998/07/how-hardwired-is-human-behavior.

4 Byron Katie, "How to Do the Work, A Guide to the Four Questions," TheWork. com, accessed April 28, 2022, https://thework.com/instruction-the-work-byron-katie/.

5 T. D. Borkovec, H. Hazlett-Stevens, and M. L. Diaz, "The Role of Positive Beliefs about Worry in Generalized Anxiety Disorder and Its Treatment," *Clinical Psychology and Psychotherapy* 6, no. 2 (May 1999): 126–138. See also this updated study that finds that individuals with Generalized Anxiety Disorder (GAD) experience "untrue worries" 91.4% of the time: LaFreniere, L. S., & Newman, M. G. (2020). "Exposing Worry's Deceit: Percentage of Untrue Worries in Generalized Anxiety Disorder Treatment." *Behavior Therapy*, 51(3), 413–423.

6 Franklin Roosevelt, "First Inaugural Address of Franklin D. Roosevelt," The Avalon Project, Lillian Goldman Law Library of Yale University, delivered March 4, 1933, accessed April 28, 2022, https://avalon.law.yale.edu/20th_century/froos1.asp.

7   *Breaking Bad,* season 2, episode 8, "Better Call Saul," directed by Terry McDonough, written by Vince Gilligan and Peter Gould, featuring Bryan Cranston, Anna Gunn, and Aaron Paul, aired April 26, 2009, on AMC.

8   Bessel van der Kolk, *The Body Keeps the Score: Brain, Mind, and Body in the Healing of Trauma* (New York: Viking Penguin, 2014), 21.

9   Daya Mata, *Finding the Joy within You: Personal Counsel for God-Centered Living* (Los Angeles: Self-Realization Fellowship, 1990), 146–147.

10   Mark Manson, "How Your Insecurity Is Bought and Sold," MarkManson.net, accessed April 28, 2022, https://markmanson.net/insecurity.

11   John-Manuel Andriote, "Legal Drug-Pushing: How Disease Mongers Keep Us All Doped Up," *Atlantic*, April 3, 2012, https://www.theatlantic.com/health/archive/2012/04/legal-drug-pushing-how-disease-mongers-keep-us-all-doped-up/255247/.

12   Beth Snyder Bulik, "Are Pharma Marketers Using Fear-Mongering Ads to Scare People into Asking for Drugs?," Fierce Pharma, September 21, 2016, https://www.fiercepharma.com/marketing/are-pharma-marketers-trying-to-scare-people-into-asking-for-drugs-fear-mongering-ads.

13   Seneca the Younger, "Letter 13, Paragraph 4," in *The Tao of Seneca: Practical Letters from a Stoic Master: Volume 1*, trans. Richard Mott Gummere (Cambridge: Harvard University Press, 2017), 67.

14   American Psychiatric Association, "Americans Say They Are More Anxious; Baby Boomers Report Greatest Increase in Anxiety," Psychiatry.org, May 6, 2018, https://www.psychiatry.org/newsroom/news-releases/americans-say-they-are-more-anxious-than-a-year-ago-baby-boomers-report-greatest-increase-in-anxiety.

15   A Chinese phrase defined in the Merriam-Webster dictionary as "one that is outwardly powerful or dangerous but inwardly weak or ineffectual."

16   Alan Watts, "Alan Watts—All That You See out in Front of You Is How You Feel inside Your Head," uploaded July 24, 2018, YouTube video, https://www.youtube.com/watch?v=D9rVbVpjk8w.

17   Adyashanti, *Emptiness Dancing* (Boulder: Sounds True, 2006), 2.

18 Seneca the Younger, "Letter 78, Paragraph 16," in *The Tao of Seneca: Practical Letters from a Stoic Master: Volume 2*, trans. Richard Mott Gummere (Cambridge: Harvard University Press, 2017), 115.

19 Adyashanti, "The Quiet Layer of Existence," uploaded December 10, 2016, YouTube video, https://www.youtube.com/watch?v=E0fsBPTYkak.

20 Anne Lamott, *Bird by Bird: Some Instructions on Writing and Life* (New York: Anchor Books, 1995), 17–18.

21 Laozi, *Daode Jing*, trans. A. Charles Muller, chap. 64, website, last modified April 26, 2021, http://www.acmuller.net/con-dao/daodejing.html.

22 "The Method," Freedman's Method Ketsugo Jujutsu, accessed April 28, 2022, https://ketsugojujutsu.com/home/.

23 Lucius Annaeus Seneca, *Hardship & Happiness*, trans. Elaine Fantham, Harry M. Hine, James Ker, and Gareth D. Williams (Chicago: University of Chicago Press, 2014), 206.

24 Plato, *Cratylus*, trans. Benjamin Jowett, Project Gutenberg e-book, released January 1999, last modified April 27, 2022, https://www.gutenberg.org/files/1616/1616-h/1616-h.htm.

25 Seneca, *On the Happy Life*, trans. Aubrey Stewart (independently published, 2017), 35.

26 Piero Ferrucci, *What We May Be* (Los Angeles: Jeremy P. Tarcher, Inc., 1982), 48.

27 Kenneth Coombs, *Tarot Alchemy: A Complete Analysis of the Major Arcana* (Bloomington: iUniverse, 2012), 1.

28 "Depersonalization-Derealization Disorder," Mayo Clinic, accessed April 28, 2022, https://www.mayoclinic.org/diseases-conditions/depersonalization-derealization-disorder/symptoms-causes/syc-20352911.

29 Swamy G, "A Blueprint to Healing from Depersonalization," *NAMI Blog*, January 8, 2020, https://www.nami.org/Blogs/NAMI-Blog/January-2020/A-Blueprint-to-Healing-From-Depersonalization.

30 Alex Williams, "Prozac Nation Is Now the United States of Xanax," *The New York Times*, June 10, 2017, https://www.nytimes.com/2017/06/10/style/anxiety-is-the-new-depression-xanax.html.

31 D. F. Santomauro, A. M. Mantilla Herrera, J. Shadid, P. Zheng, C. Ashbaugh, D. Pigott, S. I. Hay, et al., "Global Prevalence and Burden of Depressive and Anxiety Disorders in 204 Countries and Territories in 2020 Due to the COVID-19 Pandemic," *Lancet* 398, no. 10312 (November 6, 2021): P1700–P1712, https://www.thelancet.com/journals/lancet/article/PIIS0140-6736(21)02143-7/fulltext#articleInformation.

32 Byron Katie, "How to Do the Work, A Guide to the Four Questions," TheWork.com, accessed April 28, 2022, https://thework.com/instruction-the-work-byron-katie/.

33 *Concise Oxford Dictionary of Quotations*, 6th ed., ed. Susan Ratcliffe (Oxford: Oxford University Press, 2011), s.v. "Voltaire," 389.

34 *Reflections: Or, Sentences and Moral Maxims.* Project Gutenberg [ebook], October, 2005.

https://www.gutenberg.org/files/9105/9105-h/9105-h.htm, maxim #476.

35 Susan Jeffers, *Feel the Fear and Do It Anyway* (New York: Harcourt Brace Jovanovich, 1987), 27.

36 Seneca the Younger, "Letter 76, Paragraph 38," in *The Tao of Seneca: Practical Letters from a Stoic Master: Volume 2*, trans. Richard Mott Gummere (Cambridge: Harvard University Press, 2017), 102.

37 Phil Stutz and Barry Michels, *The Tools* (London: Vermillion, 2012), 66–67.

38 "Destroy Negativity From Your Mind With This Simple Exercise" *Mission.org* (blog), *Medium*, November 27, 2017, https://medium.com/the-mission/a-practical-hack-to-combat-negative-thoughts-in-2-minutes-or-less-cc3d1bddb3af

39 *Hamlet*, ed. Edmund K. Chambers (London: Blackie & Son Limited, 1894), 2.2.254–255.

40 *Handbook of Epictetus*, trans. Nicholas P. White, (Indianapolis, IN: Hackett Publishing Company, 1983).

41   Friedrich Nietzsche, *Beyond Good and Evil*, trans. Helen Zimmern (New York: The MacMillan Company, 1907), 13.

42   Jack Kornfield, *Bringing Home the Dharma* (Boston: Shambhala Publications, 2011), 104.

43   Ryan Holiday, *The Obstacle Is the Way* (New York: Portfolio/Penguin, 2014), 29.

44   William Irvine, "What Stoicism Isn't," *HuffPost*, last modified July 19, 2014, https://www.huffpost.com/entry/what-stoicism-isnt_b_5346269.

45   Julia Cameron, *The Artist's Way* (New York: Tarcher Perigee, 2016), 44.

46   Phil Stutz, "Ignite Your Inner Greatness," 33Voices, accessed April 28, 2022, https://33voices.com/interviews/ignite-your-inner-greatness/.

47   Lincoln Barnett, *The Universe and Dr. Einstein* (Mineola: Dover Publications, 1985), 19.

48   Epictetus, *The Art of Living*, trans. Sharon Lebell (New York: HarperCollins, 1995), 3.

49   Eckhart Tolle, *The Power of Now* (Novato: New World Library, 2004), 208.

50   "Overdose Death Rates," National Institute on Drug Abuse, January 20, 2022, https://nida.nih.gov/drug-topics/trends-statistics/overdose-death-rates.

51   Holly B. Shakya and Nicholas A Christakis, "Association of Facebook Use With Compromised Well-Being: A Longitudinal Study," *American Journal of Epidemiology* 185, no. 3 (February 1, 2017): 203–211, https://pubmed.ncbi.nlm.nih.gov/28093386/.

52   *The Modern Library Collection of Greek and Roman Philosophy: 3-Book Bundle* [ebook], (New York: Random House, Inc., 2002, 200, 1941), 139.

53   Sean Lawlor, "An MDMA Therapist on How It Works and Why It's Better than Current Treatments," *Rooster*, October 1, 2018, https://therooster.com/blog/an-mdma-therapist-on-how-it-works-and-why-it%e2%80%99s-better-than-current-treatments.

54   Sean Lawlor, "An MDMA Therapist on How It Works and Why It's Better than Current Treatments," *Rooster*, October 1, 2018, https://therooster.com/blog/an-mdma-therapist-on-how-it-works-and-why-it%e2%80%99s-better-than-current-treatments.

55 Kurt Hackbarth, "Healing PTSD with MDMA Therapy," *Freethink*, December 28, 2019, https://www.freethink.com/health/mdma-therapy-ptsd.

56 Megan Call, "Neuroplasticity: How to Use Your Brain's Malleability to Improve Your Well-Being," Accelerate Learning Community, August 8, 2019, https://accelerate.uofuhealth.utah.edu/resilience/neuroplasticity-how-to-use-your-brain-s-malleability-to-improve-your-well-being.

57 Celeste Campbell, "What Is Neuroplasticity?," *Brainline*, February 4, 2009, https://www.brainline.org/author/celeste-campbell/qa/what-neuroplasticity.

58 "Herbert Benson, MD," *The Connection: Mind Your Body*, accessed April 28, 2022, https://www.theconnection.tv/dr-herbert-benson-m-d/.

59 Bruce Kehr, "DNA: I Am Who I Am…or Am I?—Session Ten," *Potomac Psychiatry* (blog), accessed April 25, 2022, https://www.potomacpsychiatry.com/blog/comt-gene-test-stress-genetic-testing.

60 "Rewire Your Head, Change Your World," *Goop* (blog), accessed April 28, 2022, https://goop.com/wellness/health/rewire-your-head-change-your-world/.

61 Adyashanti, "The Quiet Layer of Existence," uploaded December 10, 2016, YouTube video, https://www.youtube.com/watch?v=E0fsBPTYkak.

62 Eckhart Tolle, "Life Is Here to Challenge All of Us," YouTube video, 7:45, May 14, 2020, https://www.youtube.com/watch?v=3fPDHvvNi_k.

63 Marcus Aurelius, "Book 7, Paragraph 56," in *Meditations: A New Translation*, trans. Gregory Hays (New York: The Modern Library, 2012), 108, Kindle.

64 KGO, "Second Chances: 'I Survived Jumping Off the Golden Gate Bridge,'" ABC 7 News, May 18, 2017, https://abc7news.com/golden-gate-bridge-suicides-suicide-survivors-jump-survive/2010562/.

65 Tae Friend, "Jumpers," *The New Yorker*, October 13, 2003, https://www.newyorker.com/magazine/2003/10/13/jumpers.

66 KGO, "Second Chances: 'I Survived Jumping Off the Golden Gate Bridge,'" ABC 7 News, May 18, 2017, https://abc7news.com/golden-gate-bridge-suicides-suicide-survivors-jump-survive/2010562/.

67 Marcus Aurelius, "Book 7, Paragraph 59," in *Meditations: A New Translation*, trans. Gregory Hays (New York: The Modern Library, 2012), 108, Kindle.

68 Christopher Volger, *The Writer's Journey*, 3rd Edition (Studio City, CA: Michael Wiese Productions, 2007), 197-98.

69 Thomas Fuller, *A Pisgah Sight of Palestine and the Confines Thereof* (London: William Tegg, 1869), 208.

70 "World Population Prospects 2019, Online Edition" United Nations Department of Economic and Social Affairs, 2019, https://population.un.org/wpp/Download/Standard/Mortality/.

71 Dōgen Zenji, *Dōgen's Extensive Record*, trans. Taigen Dan Leighton and Shohaku Okumura (Boston: Wisdom Publications, 2010), 535.

72 Ryan Holiday, *The Obstacle Is the Way* (New York: Portfolio/Penguin, 2014), 7–8.

73 Wikiquote, s.v. "Catharsis," last modified December 2, 2019, 15:56, https://en.wikiquote.org/wiki/Catharsis.